UNDERSTANDING THE CHURCH

Understanding the Church

DAVID JACKMAN

KINGSWAY PUBLICATIONS
EASTBOURNE

ISBN 0 86065 449 4

Unless otherwise indicated, biblical quotations are from
the Holy Bible: New International Version, copyright
© International Bible Society 1973, 1978, 1984.

Front cover design by Vic Mitchell

Printed in Great Britain for
KINGSWAY PUBLICATIONS LTD
Lottbridge Drove, Eastbourne, E. Sussex BN23 6NT by
Richard Clay Ltd, Bungay, Suffolk.
Typeset by CST, Eastbourne, E. Sussex.

To
all the members and congregation of
Above Bar Church, Southampton,
from whom and with whom
I have learned so much.

Contents

Introduction

This book began its life in the autumn of 1983. At that time the church was being forced to come to terms with a number of practical challenges as a result of fairly rapid growth. This was evidenced in the numbers attending our Sunday worship services and who through that initial connection wanted to be involved in a variety of different ways in the life and work of the church. Many of these newcomers had only the haziest of church backgrounds or knowledge about the Christian faith. Some had been brought up to go to Sunday School or had attended church youth groups years ago, but had no adult experience of a living faith. Others had imbibed a number of false ideas about the nature of real Christianity and had a good deal of 'un-learning' to do before they were ready to turn to Christ. It was important for them, as for the continuing nucleus of the congregation, that we all understood the nature of the church, so that we could establish together God's priorities and principles for our fellowship and service.

For seventy-five years or more now there has been a strong biblical witness to the reality of Jesus Christ as Saviour and Lord on our church site, in the centre of the city of Southampton. Known first as the Church of Christ and later as Above Bar Church (taking its name from the main shopping street, in which it stands, north of the old city Bargate) the church was served for nearly seventy years by two outstanding and greatly loved pastors, Frederick Phillips and Leith Samuel. When I succeeded the latter in 1980 the church was in the midst of an exciting rebuilding project. In the summer of 1979 the Victorian building, just short of its century, was razed to the ground and a completely new project was begun. The church complex which emerged extends for three floors, above two shops, which look onto the street, and in this way in co-operation with a property developer the value of the site was released for the advantage of the church. With a lounge and hall at the front; offices, classrooms and a basement hall at the back, the worship area seating 650 people and built on an amphitheatre model became the filling of the sandwich in the middle, extending the full height of the building above the shops. Robert Potter, a Christian architect based in Southampton, who had among many other church projects designed the Millmead Centre in Guildford and the reconstruction of All Souls' Langham Place, produced a building of distinction and versatility, for which we never cease to thank God.

For over two years the congregation experienced a peripatetic existence; on Sunday mornings at the largest lecture theatre in the University Medical School and on Sunday evenings in the Mountbatten Theatre at the local College of Technology. We were the grateful guests of several other local churches who put their premises at our disposal for additional special events. The most significant factor, however, was that from the moment we left the old building the congregation began to grow – slowly while the rebuilding project developed, but then much more quickly when once the new building had been opened in September 1981. That steady growth has continued until the present time. Undoubtedly the interest generated in the building project was a major advantage in bringing the church before the public. The local media served us very well and there was considerable interest in a new church being built in the city centre, for the first time in decades. The building itself is warm and welcoming, pleasantly equipped and furnished, without being lavish, so that anyone can quickly feel at home in its contemporary environment. But none of these physical assets can adequately account for the growth which God has been bringing about. Nor is it growth that has been planned through a carefully researched programme or detailed application of church growth principles, much as I have come to value both tools. It is as we have applied ourselves to trying to understand what God is doing, in our local context, that we have been driven back again and again to the New Testament to rediscover our bearings and to reassess our programmes and priorities against God's yardstick.

That is really why this book was written. It comes out of a very specific, local church situation, with all the particularity and limitations attendant on that. But, in visiting again the principles on which all life and growth occur, within the body of Christ, it is my prayer that we shall become in practice what we affirm we long to be—a biblical church, governed by and obedient to God's word. At the heart of Above Bar's ministry lies the Bible. We believe that the Spirit of God still uses the word of God (the whole Bible) to produce and to bring to maturity the children of God. The Scriptures are still our supreme authority in all matters of faith and conduct because we believe in their divine inspiration and therefore their inerrancy.

This is reflected in our Sunday worship services, in which the hearing and preaching of God's word is a central ingredient. While we are told that people today are either unwilling to, or incapable of, listening for more than ten to fifteen minutes to a sermon, we find the exact opposite to be true. With not far short of a thousand different people attending our three Sunday services at present, the vast majority would say that what they value most is the Bible teaching they receive, together with the real love and warmth of the church family, expressed in practical care and support. This is not a matter of intellectualism, of being overly cerebral or even (worse smear!) middle-class, which are all grounds on which serious Bible preaching is summarily dismissed today. My own congregation is a cross-section of the city, with people from a wide variety of backgrounds finding that the word of God properly taught and relevantly applied speaks with equal penetration to all sorts and conditions of men, women and young people.

Nor is this a matter of a pulpit personality cult, as can be seen by the fact that wherever the Bible is taught in a faithful, consistent, but warm-hearted, lively and above all relevant way, churches are growing. All around us thousands of men and women want to know whether there is any word from the Lord, yet all too often if ever they enter a church the last thing they hear is authoritative biblical teaching. Too many churches and ministers have lost their nerve in this area, with devastating results. Church life becomes an endless quest for the latest gimmicks or popular attractions to fill the vacuum that results. 'Roller-coaster' Christianity takes over and the congregation is rapidly destabilized.

But when we do get back to the Bible we find that we are given our continuing priorities with astonishing insistence and clarity. Christ expects the church to grow. Small is not necessarily beautiful, when the church has been given a world-wide commission that is still unfulfilled. We discover that the priorities of the Head of the church are the making and maturing of disciples—evangelism and edification—so that all we devote so much time to, in our busy church schedules, needs to be assessed by what Jesus tells us actually matters most to him. The Bible challenges us to look at our church life from God's perspective, which does not always (or often) necessarily coincide with the latest fashions in the Christian media, much less the dominant preoccupations of our secular culture. We need a frequent corrective to our 'this-worldliness' by resolutely facing the stringent demands of Scripture to judge our culture by God's unchanging truth. Whether or not those who claim to be prophets today actually speak God's word can be very hard to determine, but at least there is no uncertainty about the content of what God has once said, and therefore still says, in the pages of the Bible.

This is not to beg the interpretative questions, which must always exercise us, but to plead that we start taking the Bible seriously again in our church life. In many church situations Christians do not hit anything because they are aiming nowhere in particular. Systematic consecutive exposition of the Scripture, chapter by chapter, week by week, corrects that imbalance.

Although our own regular Sunday practice is to preach through a different book of the Bible, morning and evening, balancing Old Testament, gospels and epistles with our house group study meetings, this book represents a number of key passages on the church, drawn from all over the New Testament. The method is the same, however, in that in each passage my aim is to draw out the major threads of teaching, to see how they relate to each other and to our own contemporary situation. Only in this way are we likely to begin to understand God's priorities for his church, and then to affirm and adhere to these, however strongly the winds of change may try to blow us off course.

Why is there not more thorough biblical teaching today? Could it be because the cost is too great, in terms of energy, time and resources? It does take many hours of prayer and study, rightly to prepare a passage of the Bible, in order to be able to teach it helpfully to others. But isn't that what the ministry is all about—ministry of the word? Churches need to set their ministers free from all the peripheral tasks of administration in order to devote themselves, as the apostles did, to prayer and the ministry of the word (Acts 6:4). When we take seriously Paul's pastoral epistles we find his great concern for the future of the churches in the post-apostolic age is that the ministry of God's word will be firmly established as the central core of the church's life and progress.

Some of our current church preoccupations are notably conspicuous by their absence, in contrast. I do not personally believe that this can be written off as 'another time, another place'. Such a view paralyses church growth and condemns us to a continuing spiritual immaturity. Of course, no one church has all the answers. Of course, every church is far from perfect and I am only too aware of the imperfections of my own church for which I bear a large slice of the responsibility. But this book is sent out with the hope and prayer that it may be used by God to help us to listen again to his word and to start to seek again his understanding of our church. If it does anything to renew our appetite, confidence in and commitment to living and proclaiming God's word, perhaps its publication will not have been in vain.

DAVID JACKMAN

I

Our Business Is Growing

Then the eleven disciples went to Galilee, to the mountain where Jesus had told them to go. When they saw him, they worshipped him; but some doubted. Then Jesus came to them and said, 'All authority in heaven and on earth has been given to me. Therefore go and make disciples of all nations, baptising them in the name of the Father and of the Son and of the Holy Spirit, and teaching them to obey everything I have commanded you. And surely I will be with you always, to the very end of the age' (Mt 28:16–20).

These challenging and exciting words are often called the Great Commission. They are the marching orders of the church, given from the lips of the Lord Jesus himself and recorded for us as the conclusion of Matthew's gospel. I want to call them the job description of the church.

We must start with the most fundamental question of all: why does the church exist? What is God's purpose in leaving his people here in this world? Immediately you became a Christian God could have translated you into his presence, and taken you into glory. You would be with Christ which, Paul says in his epistle to the Philippians, is 'far better'. But God chooses not to do that. He leaves his church in the world, a decision that affects us all, in our personal lives, as families and as communities. For that key decision by God is going to dictate the major way in which we spend our lives. It determines what we do with our resources, our time, talents, money and much else besides. It decides our priorities and makes us ask ourselves what we are really living for. Why are we here as the church of God?

Quite clearly, as Christians we do not exist in the world primarily to make our living or to provide material security for ourselves and our children. Nor is our major purpose to uphold the democratic way of life, nor even to save our nation from moral and spiritual decay. That does not mean that Christians should have no earthly concerns. Of course we are to provide for our families, and to be concerned for our community by being actively involved in it, as Christ's salt and light. Of course we should be the best citizens we can be, while recognizing that our citizenship ultimately is not here at all, but in heaven. But all that is not the basic purpose for our being in the world. The Bible sees us as pilgrims, who are passing through. We are 'resident aliens', whose right of abode is elsewhere. That is to say, we do not really belong *finally* to this world. So what in the world are Christians for?

Jesus leaves us in no doubt about it. At the heart of those demanding words with which he commissioned his church, there is one imperative that stands out as the main verb, the command to 'make disciples'. And related to that command there are three present participles that indicate how it is to be carried out: 'going . . . baptising . . . teaching'. This is so clear that if you had said to those eleven disciples, 'What did the Lord say when he gave you the agenda for the future? What did he commission his church on earth to do?', they would reply that they were to go everywhere and win men to Christ. They were to baptize them, as the outward testimony of their personal, inward faith and to teach them all the truth, as it is in Jesus.

Disciples are learners. That is what the word means, but not just learners in an academic sense. They had to learn not only the content of Christ's commands and teaching, but also to obey him, to do whatever he said. It is only too easy to concentrate on the head knowledge, but we do not really understand spiritual truth, in the depths of our beings, until we start to practise it. That was the programme for the early church, as we shall see in the forthcoming chapters.

Now all the other things we have to do in our earthly lives may well be good, proper and right concerns—family concerns, business matters, and all sorts of legitimate calls upon our time—but our priority as Christians is to see others becoming Christ's disciples. That is why the church is here in the world. And that is why in Acts 1:8 the Lord Jesus spoke to the disciples again, just before his ascension, and promised them, 'You will receive power when the Holy Spirit comes on you; and you will be my witnesses.'

The power that the Holy Spirit gives to every believer in Jesus is a power to witness to the reality of Christ as Saviour and Lord, and so to fulfil the marching orders of the church. There is no power to witness effectively apart from God, the Holy Spirit. Then, and only then, could the disciples be Christ's witnesses, firstly in Jerusalem, then in all Judea, Samaria and ultimately to the ends of the earth. That is what the Great Commission means; the church is to go to all nations, starting in Jerusalem and reaching out to the ends of the earth.

We can study one example of how that worked out in the early church, one that shows that this was an emphasis they did not forget. We read in Acts 14: 21–22 that Paul and Barnabas preached the good news in Derbe and won a large number of disciples there. Then they returned to Lystra, Iconium and Antioch, where they had previously preached, strengthening the disciples and encouraging them to remain true to the faith. The verses stress their teaching that 'We must go through many hardships to enter the kingdom of God'.

Luke is showing us what the church was actually doing at that stage. They were preaching the gospel and winning not just converts but *disciples*, people who were learners of Jesus and were committed to him. But neither was that enough on its own. They also returned to the places where they had already evangelized and went on to strengthen the disciples. They encouraged them to remain true to the faith. They were fulfilling the Lord's command to make disciples by preaching the gospel; going, baptizing and teaching converts to observe all that he had commanded. So they 'discipled' (it is exactly the same verb as that used in Matthew 28).

From this we can derive the two dominant ingredients in the life of the early church. They were evangelism and edification, or, if you prefer it in other terms, outreach and up-building—but both things together. They were reaching out, making disciples and then helping them to grow, building people into the image of Christ. It is important to underline again that the two agencies by which this was achieved were the word of Christ in the gospel ('all that I have commanded you') and the Spirit of Christ, the 'dynamic' or power to witness, the divine ability to get the job done. Both are indispensable, and both belong together, today as much as then. That remains the agenda for every local church, every community of disciples. We are to grow in our faith and to build one another up so that increasingly we obey all that the Lord has commanded us.

I once saw the title of this chapter on a delivery van for a market gardener, and it seemed to me to be such an appropriate motto for the church—'Our business is growing'. It is our business to grow numerically, as the number of disciples increases through the church's evangelism. That should be the norm where a congregation is taking the Great Commission seriously and prayerfully. But it is also our business to grow in quality as disciples, as each of us becomes more like the Lord Jesus. Both sorts of growth are vital and biblical requirements. There must be expansion as disciples are made; there must also be a deepening of spiritual life.

It is important to remember that because these two strands of outreach and up-building run through the whole of the New Testament they do not work against each other. There are some people who are terribly worried about evangelism being given too high a priority on the church's agenda, fearing that if we become too tied up with those who are not yet Christians we will not then be able to give enough time to care for one another. There are churches, however, where so much emphasis is placed on pastoral work that their backs are turned to the world and there is no outreach. The members become like a circle of children, all holding hands and looking inwards. But rightly and biblically understood, the two complement each other.

Before we go into more detail in these chapters, it is worth your asking yourself if you actually believe these things. Are they your personal priorities? Does your church have these priorities at the top of its agenda? Do you judge all you do as a church against these yardsticks? I ask this, because I have found many Christians who imagine that a growing church will become overconcerned with numbers, when looking for the spectacular in the sense of bigger and better things, as though they were an end in themselves. As my own church was experiencing quite rapid growth, we had to face the feeling on the part of some members that it was now quite big enough and we ought to settle down with what we had. I was even accused of being obsessed with evangelism! I regard that as a very great compliment, which I hope and pray will be true for us all, because one day I have to give an account to

God of my stewardship, and so do you. Whatever our role within the church—and every member has a gift to be used and a ministry to be fulfilled—we are ultimately responsible to our Master, as individual stewards, for our use of the talents he has given to us. The head of the church is the Lord of the harvest. And the scripture leaves us in no doubt as to what he will say to those who put their comfort before his kingdom, to those who buried their talents and opted for safety and security when he called us to a life of adventurous obedience in his service. As the church of the Lord Jesus Christ, we have not been called merely to preserve the status quo. Our business is growing, and if we do not have a heart for the lost then we do not have the heart of Christ. Our Lord was deeply moved with compassion for the crowds whom he saw as sheep without a shepherd (Mt 9:36-38). Our Lord wept over Jerusalem, as the people of that privileged city turned their backs on him (Lk 19:41). And if we are unwilling to become more like him, what right have we to call ourselves his disciples? 'Go and make disciples of all nations, baptising them . . . and teaching them to obey everything.'

I am placing much emphasis on evangelism in this chapter because it is foundational to the theme of the book as a whole. So let us go back to the text of Matthew 28 and consider the content of what our Lord is saying in these verses. Verse 18: 'Jesus came to them and said, "All authority in heaven and on earth has been given to me."' That is the first of four occasions on which the word 'all' or 'everything' occurs in these verses. Firstly, Jesus claims that *all* authority belongs to him. As we saw earlier, Christ is the head of the church and the Lord of all, so that every one of us as a disciple is personally responsible to him. He has risen from the dead and he is eternally alive. The earliest and most basic Christian Creed is 'Jesus is Lord'. All authority belongs to Jesus. You and I know that we cannot be Christians without submitting personally to his lordship in our lives. If he is not Lord, then we are living a lie as Christians. He rules both on earth and in heaven, so he is to rule in the lives of his people. Either we recognize his authority and we become disciples, or we live in rebellion against the greatest reality of the universe, which is the lordship of Jesus Christ. There are no two ways about it. Furthermore, that authority has been given, Jesus says, by God the Father as the direct result of the Son's perfect fulfilment of the Father's will, culminating in Christ's death on the cross.

All authority always belongs to Jesus because, from before time began, Jesus was co-equal in the Trinity with the Father. But in a special way, that authority was given back into the hands of the Christ who was about to ascend to heaven, because of his great work in making our redemption possible, through his death on the cross and by his glorious resurrection. It is in the name of the God who made and owns the world, and under the supreme authority of Jesus Christ, to whom every knee will bow, that we are commanded therefore to go. There is no choice. In effect, he says to his disciples, 'Mine is the authority and I am therefore telling you to do something. Make disciples.' He put for all time the onus upon his church to go and share her faith with other people, to go and be channels of his love and his truth in his lost world.

It is interesting that in the New Testament we do not find the church holding services and expecting those who are not yet believers to come to them. Always, they were prepared to go and share the good news, whether in the synagogue, the market-place, or in people's homes. Too often we have been construed by the world simply to be saying, 'Come and get it.' Jesus said, 'Go and give it.' Their confidence was that all authority belonged to their Lord. They were under his orders and that was why they were able to be so bold. That too is why they went so joyfully. So the mission of the church is the direct result of the lordship of Christ.

The second 'all' refers to the destination of the ministry. We are to go and make disciples of *all* nations (verse 19). In others words, it is the purpose of Jesus that his church should spread so widely that every nation is represented among the number of his disciples. In one sense, the whole story of the Bible is the story of the church, because it is central to God's purpose for his world, throughout history, and he is calling out a people for himself, in every generation. When Israel first became a nation God promised to his people, 'I will be your God and you will be my people.' In one of the first covenant promises in the Bible given to Abraham in Genesis 12:1-3 God says, 'I will make you into a great nation and I will bless you,' but then goes on to add, 'and all peoples on earth will be blessed through you.' From the start, there was no narrowness in God's vision. He does not simply promise to bless Abraham and through him the nation of Israel, but rather that he will bless the *whole* of his world through what he does for Abraham and his descendants. God is never thought of in the Old Testament as a tribal deity, limited to Israel. He is the God of the whole world. That is the great unifying theme of scripture, that the good news is seen to be spreading throughout the whole earth.

It is a theme that comes to its glorious climax in the book of Revelation, which looks forward to the fulfilment of all that has been promised. The apostle John is being granted a glimpse into heaven, and he sees a great multitude that no one could count; people from every nation, tribe, people and language, standing before the throne and in front of the Lamb (Rev 7:9). 'They were wearing white robes and were holding palm branches in their hands. And they cried out in a loud voice: "Salvation belongs to our God, who sits on the throne, and to the Lamb"' (verse 10). That is the fulfilment of what God promised in

Genesis 12:3. All that was promised to Abraham came to fruition in Christ, through whom all the nations were blessed in inheriting what was promised. That inheritance is redeemed men and women who constitute the church, the body of Christ, so that the church in heaven will be a great multitude, from every nation. This means that you cannot be a biblical Christian unless you think centrally about the church and about our worldwide mission. Furthermore, we must remember that our mission is not to influence, or to impress, but to see all nations discipled. That is Christ's concern—to call out a universal family of God's children, from every kindred and tongue, those whom he has made his disciples.

All this, of course, implies a radical change in lifestyle, because the disciple is, as we saw earlier, a learner of Jesus. If you and I are going to become learners of Jesus, it means we are going to receive his word, believe it and also to do it. He gave an outward badge of this discipleship in the ordinance of baptism, 'baptizing them' in the name of the Trinity. For baptism is the outward sign of belonging to Christ, the external expression that I have died to my old self-centred way of living and have freely and gladly resigned myself to the control of Jesus Christ as my Lord. I have become a new person in Christ, raised in him to new life and I am not ashamed for all the world to know that I am his disciple. Baptism is the outward physical sign of this inward spiritual grace, which is why the New Testament knows nothing about unbaptized disciples. Not that we become disciples by being baptized, but it is God's appointed means by which we testify to our union with Christ, whose stated goal is to see men and women of all nations discipled and baptized.

The third 'all' in Matthew 28 is there in verse 20, 'Teaching them to obey *everything* [all] I have command-ed you.' All authority, all nations, all commands. Jesus says there is to be a comprehensiveness about Christian teaching if his church is to grow. Nothing must be omitted from Christ's instructions. Therefore, teaching is a very important ingredient in the life and ministry of any church. But the teaching is not merely with the aim of acquiring a body of Christian knowledge. Jesus makes this clear in verse 20: 'teaching them'—not just to learn everything I have commanded, or to make notes on everything I have commanded, but 'to obey everything I have commanded'. It is not wrong to make notes of what you learn, but you should do so with a view to obey. Teaching must be applied in our lives and worked out in practice. Most of us, as Christians, face our problems not so much in the area of knowing what we *ought* to do, as in actually carrying out Christ's instructions. That is why we fail to grow. He wants his disciples to obey it all. Perhaps the very area that is in your mind as you read these words could be the thing he wants to change and to work on in your life, to make you more like himself, so that you can grow as a Christian. The logic is that if there is an area in which we are not obeying Christ, we are blocking him out from that part of our lives, and this quenches and grieves the Holy Spirit so that our development and our blessing in many other areas is hindered. But the sort of growth of character and Christlikeness that God looks for in all of us can only be the fruit of obedience.

The Bible evaluates spiritual maturity not only by what we believe, but by how we live. Too often, we measure our spiritual depth and reality by externals. If a Christian does not do certain 'worldly' things, then he is automatically classified as spiritual. That, of course, is the same sickness from which the Pharisees suffered. It can develop into a man-made legalism. What Jesus said is that we have to obey everything that *he* commanded, which does not mean that we are obliged to obey all the rules of the Christian subculture which other Christians have constructed. It also means that it is possible to refrain from many sins, and yet to become proud, hard and critical of other people. We are not really being obedient. What about the command to show real love and compassion to fellow Christians who are in need, who have fallen into sin, or who have some other kind of problem? What about your concern for those who do not yet know Christ? 'Obey *everything* I have commanded you.' And that is an obligation that will extend throughout our lives, as we are continually seeing new areas in which we are to become obedient. Both licence on the one hand, and legalism on the other, are errors; but Christ commands us clearly in his word that there are certain authority statements for us to live by.

Lastly, at the end of verse 20, he reminds us, 'I will be with you *always* [all the days], to the very end of the age.' All authority, all nations, all commands, all the days. This gives us a time perspective that we may find hard to grasp. The growth of the church will only stop when Christ returns at the end of the age. We are used to somebody growing and stopping. We see plants growing in our garden. They have a season of growth and then they cease. They do not go on indefinitely, except for the weeds! But this other sort of growing does, at least until the end of time. The church is growing continually. And that is why even though these words were actually spoken to the apostles, they still relate to us today, because Jesus knew perfectly well that those apostles would be in heaven long before the end of the age.

This is for the church in every generation. Christ is with his people every day, in every situation, with every opportunity. Just as his authority is our confidence, so his presence is our strength. We go in his name. But the experience of Christ being with us is always linked to our obedience in going. Make disciples and you will find that Christ is with you. Reach out in his name and you will find he is there. Obey what he has taught you and you will know his presence always to the very end of the age. And the church that is on the move, growing and growing, is the church that especially knows the Lord is with them. 'Our business is growing.' What could be more exciting, or eternally worthwhile, than that?

And so I find God challenging my heart as I begin this book. I pray he challenges yours as you read it to say, 'Am I going to be a disciple, or just a spectator? Am I going to be a worker, or a shirker? Am I going to be a committed Christian, or just a critic who looks on from the outside?' We shall give an account to him one day of what we have done with the life he has given us. He has not left us in any doubt about his priorities. Let us say to him today in the quietness of our hearts, 'Lord, help me to trust and obey.'

2

Three Case Studies in Growth

In the last chapter we saw Christ's comprehensive agenda for his church—make disciples so that the church might grow. Now we need to study how that plan began to work out in practice, so in this chapter we look at three case studies taken from the book of Acts.

Before we go on to look at these passages in detail, however, we need some basic introduction. As you turn to the pages of Acts, it is instructive to notice the significant difference in atmosphere between the New Testament church at work in the world and much of our twentieth century church experience. One of the most significant things about the New Testament, whether in the Acts of the Apostles, or the epistles, is that the apostolic leaders were not continually exhorting the church to subscribe more money for missionary work. They were not continually repeating the Great Commission and urging it on the reluctant Christians, to fulfil the duty of evangelism. In fact, if you go to the epistles and try to find a passage that stirs up Christians to evangelize, you would be very hard put to find anything at all. The obvious reason must be because the church was evangelizing naturally.

True evangelism is overflow. If you drink deeply of the

water of life in Jesus, he has said that out of your innermost being will flow rivers of living water (Jn 7:37, 38). But this only happens in those who come to him and drink, so that the apostles do not spend time trying to beat the church up into a frenzy of activity. Instead, Acts provides a series of notes that tell us what was happening. We can start with Acts 2:1-41—the day of Pentecost, which many people have called the birthday of the church. Those who accepted Peter's message that day were baptized and about 3,000 were added to their number. The church from the very beginning is growing. Then we see in Acts 2: 47, 'And the Lord added to their number daily those who were being saved.' Again in Acts 6:7; 'So the word of God spread. The number of disciples in Jerusalem increased rapidly and a large number of priests became obedient to the faith.' The gospel is not just spreading but penetrating. The church is growing because there are Christians who are drinking of the Lord Jesus to overflowing.

By Acts 9:31 we read that it had spread throughout Judea and into Galilee and Samaria as well, and that the growing church enjoyed a time of peace. It was strengthened and, encouraged by the Holy Spirit, grew in numbers, living in the fear of the Lord. The Acts of the Apostles expects the church to grow, as new believers are added all the time when the Holy Spirit is at work, through Christians who drink deeply of Jesus. Acts 12:24, 'The word of God continued to increase and spread.' Acts 13:49, 'The Word of the Lord spread through the whole region.' And Acts 16:5, 'So the churches were strengthened in the faith and grew daily in numbers.'

Luke does not overemphasize the point. He does not say, 'Now I'm going to tell you something very extraordinary.' There is just a little note here and there to indicate that the church is growing and spreading, the implication being as one would expect. Every day people are becoming Christians. But do we expect the same today? This is what I mean about the difference between the first and the twentieth century churches. We spend considerable time and energy on trying to stir people up to evangelize within the twentieth century church, whereas within the first century church there seems to have been a spontaneity about it, an ingredient that we often sadly lack. I am, of course, not against mass evangelism, provided the message is biblical and provided there is no compromise of the truth in any co-operation with others. But we are not to rely upon so-called mass evangelism, nor are we to imagine that it can stand alone without personal evangelism. The early church spread by ordinary Christians 'overflowing Jesus'.

The classic passage is found in Acts 8:1-4 which underlines my point. It was the ordinary Christians sharing the faith, who made the church grow. As the great persecution broke out against the Jerusalem church following the martyrdom of Stephen, all except the apostles scattered throughout Judea and Samaria. The apostles, the professionals if you like, stayed in Jerusalem, but ordinary Christians had to run for their lives. So what happened? Did they do what you might expect and hide in caves or go underground? Did they begin to deny their faith and decide to go off to some other town and forget about it all? Not at all. Look at Acts 8:4. 'Those who had been scattered [that is, the ordinary Christians, not the apostles] preached the word wherever they went.' As Dr Martyn Lloyd-Jones once paraphrased it: 'They gossiped the gospel wherever they went.'

That is why the church grew and there is no other way that the church will grow, until Christians 'overflow' Jesus to other people and until it becomes natural for us to share the good news with people to whom we build bridges of friendship in most ordinary ways. As the believers settled into their new situations, having to make a new living in

places they had not been before, they met people; as the
opportunity arose they doubtless shared why they were
there.

'Why have you come from Jerusalem?' they were asked.

'Well, we are Christians,' they replied, or to be histori-
cally accurate, 'We are followers of the Way.'

'Which way?'

'Not so much which, as who! The Way is a person.
Jesus is the Way.'

And so they shared Christ and the word of God spread.

We see in all this that God had his plans for the gospel.
His method of getting the church to evangelize was
persecution. It was because of the persecution in Jerusalem
that they were scattered everywhere and took the gospel
with them. That needs to be thought about. It indicates
how foundational is God's concern that his word should
spread and that his people be gathered from all nations,
through the communication of the gospel.

The book of Acts was written for the same reason as the
Old Testament histories, so that we might learn the
unchanging spiritual principles of God's work. Even
though our world is so different, the Holy Spirit can teach
us the principles of the way in which God works and
wants us to be acting in co-operation with him, in order
for his word to spread and for his church to grow. As you
probably know, church growth experts distinguish, I
think usefully, three different types of growth. A church
can grow biologically, that is to say, the children in it
grow up and become Christians and are added to the
church. It can also grow by transfer, by people moving
into a city or town, deciding it is the place God wants
them to be and then becoming members of that local
congregation. They are already Christians, but they
transfer. Thirdly, a church can grow by conversion, that is
by people becoming Christians for the first time. Our
biological and transfer growth are important, but

obviously if the church is to grow absolutely it must be by conversion growth, and that is what we must be especially concerned to see. We can see this in Acts 11 in the story of the church in Antioch, which is our first study.

> Now those who had been scattered by the persecution in connection with Stephen travelled as far as Phoenicia, Cyprus and Antioch, telling the message only to Jews. Some of them, however, men from Cyprus and Cyrene, went to Antioch and began to speak to Greeks also, telling them the good news about the Lord Jesus. The Lord's hand was with them, and a great number of people believed and turned to the Lord. News of this reached the ears of the church at Jerusalem, and they sent Barnabas to Antioch. When he arrived and saw the evidence of the grace of God, he was glad and encouraged them all to remain true to the Lord with all their hearts. He was a good man, full of the Holy Spirit and faith, and a great number of people were brought to the Lord. Then Barnabas went to Tarsus to look for Saul, and when he found him, he brought him to Antioch. So for a whole year Barnabas and Saul met with the church and taught great numbers of people. The disciples were first called Christians at Antioch (Acts 11:19-26).

This was a church that grew through a ministry to interested Gentiles. Perhaps God-fearers would be a better term, for there were some Greeks who rejected the paganism of their culture and who, although they had never been circumcised as Jewish proselytes, were yet to some degree in touch with the Jewish synagogues as worshippers of the one true God. It seems as though it is likely that these Jewish Christians began to reach out first of all to the God-fearing Greeks, people who were on the fringe of things, interested but not committed. Now how was the gospel going to reach them?

The church began in Israel, in Jerusalem, where the local population would have been among the most conservative of the Jewish people. The Christians in Israel retained their conservatism in their commitment to Hebrew culture and thought–forms, even after their conversions. But it was to this Jerusalem church that the Commission was given to go to all nations and preach the gospel. It is important to remember how difficult this was for the Jerusalem Christians to accept. They would say, 'Salvation is of the Jews.' Remember how Peter in Acts 10 had to be persuaded, by a vision from the Lord, that it was acceptable, indeed required by God, for him to share the gospel with the Gentiles. God prepared the way for him to minister to the Roman centurion, Cornelius, through a vision of the animals that were unclean to the Jews, coming down in a sheet, and by telling him, 'Get up, Peter. Kill and eat.' Peter's initial response was, 'I have never eaten anything impure or unclean' (verse 14), but God taught him through this that he had not separated off the Gentile nations, but that he wanted them to be brought into his kingdom too.

Peter took a lot of convincing, and he was not alone in that. The Jerusalem church was not naturally a missionary church bursting to reach out to all the nations, so God employed a drastic method, because he is committed to world evangelization. He scattered the Jerusalem church to Phoenicia (what we now call Lebanon), to Cyprus, to Syria and to Antioch. But, when the church scattered around these areas, which are so familiar to us now through the daily news, they told the message only to Jews. It was clearly not the Jerusalem Christians who began to evangelize the Gentiles. Acts 11: 20 explains that some of the men from Cyprus and Cyrene went to Antioch and began to speak to Greeks also. The Christians who started to evangelize the Gentiles were Jews, not from Jerusalem, but from Gentile areas. They came from a culture in which they had constant links through business with Gentile people. Naturally, they were much more cosmopolitan in their outlook than the Jerusalem Christians and therefore much better equipped to build natural bridges of friendship to interested Gentiles. So what we find in verse 20 is a group of businessmen in Antioch, who set out to reach their colleagues with the good news of Jesus.

That, then, is how this church in Antioch grew. They began to speak daily about Christ as they had the opportunity, but the growth happened spontaneously. Nobody set up a tent in the middle of Antioch and called in a preacher. It was simply that these Christians could not keep quiet. They had to share with others the joy that they had found because, as we all know, news is always difficult to keep secret, especially if it is good news. As they experienced the wonderful power and presence of Jesus in their lives, and as they drank deeply of him, they just had to tell somebody—they 'overflowed'. Of course, it was more than just a natural instinct, because the Holy Spirit was in them, the same Holy Spirit who longs and strives for men and women to come and know Christ for themselves.

The Holy Spirit's great work in the world is to take the things of Jesus and to make them real and precious to people. He yearns for men and women to be saved. That is in his nature and function, so when he is working in us as Christians, one of the clearest evidences of his fullness is that we too long for other people to be converted. We long to share the good news of the gospel with them and we delight when there are opportunities to overflow.

So what happened? Look again at verse 20. They told them the good news about Jesus and especially about his lordship. The people who heard turned to the Lord (verse 21) and so a great number of people were brought to him (verse 24). Thus, the content of what we communicate is of vital importance, and this point can be made about all three of the churches we are looking at. They did not simply make friends. They did not just share their experiences or merely invite people to church—there wasn't one to invite them to! They did not present the truth in a half-hearted, embarrassed way. They proclaimed the lordship of Jesus Christ as the greatest news in the world. And when that happens a church will grow.

Let us at this point be honest with ourselves before God, and ask ourselves how often, in the recent past, we have done that, in any way at all. So often we have become so defensive, so apologetic (in the wrong sense), so hesitant, with the result that the Lord's hand is not with us. Verse 21 makes it clear that his hand was with the believers from Cyprus and Cyrene as they went, telling the good news.

When he gave the Great Commission, Jesus said that it is as you *go* that he is with you. If we are not obeying that Commission, then we need to ask God to forgive us, for evangelism is something that depends upon drinking deeply of Jesus Christ every day. If I have no real concern for other people and if nothing of Christ overflows from my life, then there is something fundamentally wrong with my Christianity. There is no chance of overflow if the tank is half-empty, or if the channel is blocked. But where there are people who look for opportunities and tell the good news, there the Lord's hand is with them, so that a 'great number' of people may believe and turn to the Lord.

I love the little phrases that Luke uses in Acts, such as 'a great number'. Would these businessmen have been flummoxed by the sheer number of converts? Would they complain, 'But we haven't got our discipleship classes sorted out yet; we can't really cope with all these people'? The danger today is that we can organize the Holy Spirit out of business, because of the high premium we place on our technology and systems. God's rushing mighty wind has a way of overwhelming our resources and breaking down our carefully controlled channels. Of course, there is an important balance here. It is equally possible for a church to be unprepared, untrained or ill-equipped for growth and that can have an equally serious inhibiting effect on what the Spirit is wanting to do. It is a matter of where we put our confidence. Let us have all the help and training we can get, but not put our reliance on these rather than on the living God. When the Lord's hand was with them in Antioch, then a great number of people believed and turned to him.

Notice the sort of response that Luke documents here: they believed and turned. You see, what these Christians were doing in their evangelism involved the *whole* man. The people they spoke to were not just influenced or impressed; their minds were gripped by the truth they had heard. Their whole lives were re-directed by it. That word 'turn' reminds us of the word 'repentance', which means a turn around, a change of mind that produces a change of direction. They turned from themselves in repentance, and to God in faith, submitting their lives to Christ as their Saviour and their Lord; that is what making disciples involves. The good news is that Jesus is Lord. That is what makes a church—when people submit to the lordship of Christ and are built into his body.

Upon that foundation let us note very briefly how the pattern of growth continued, because that was not the end of it. Barnabas was sent down from Jerusalem (verse 22) since the Antioch believers needed to be taught. He saw evidence (verse 23) of the grace of God in the fact that they confessed Christ as Lord. When I confess this, I mean not just that Jesus is pepping me up and I lean on him occasionally for a little bit of an injection of extra help, but that I have submitted my life to him. He is directing the way it goes and I am doing what he commands.

Barnabas saw that quality in Antioch. But rather than trying to stereotype their development, with a long list of dos and don'ts, he shares their joy and encourages them to remain true to the Lord with all their hearts. His ministry was on the great essentials, and his life was an example to them, a man whose heart was full of the Holy Spirit and faith. He teaches them to 'cleave to the Lord with all your heart', to hold on to him with everything you have, because conversion must be followed and authenticated by continuance. Your daily walk with God depends on the daily openness to Christ, living by the power of the Spirit, through faith in Christ's resources and drawing on all that Christ himself is. If new Christians are to grow, there has to be that humble, but firm, determination to live Christ's way.

'He [Barnabas] was a good man, full of the Holy Spirit and faith, and a great number of people were brought to the Lord' (verse 24). That is the biblical pattern for church growth. An initial group of people are converted (verse 21). Barnabas disciples them, and then through *their* ministry a great number of other people are brought to the Lord. The result is a church that is already growing, because people see the real change in their friends' lives, and it becomes magnetic. It amazes them. Yet Barnabas, whose special gift is encouraging, recognizes that you just cannot go on building a church on encouragement alone. People have to be taught as well; so he travels to Tarsus to look for Paul. After what is probably quite a long time, he finds him and brings him back to Antioch. There, Barnabas and Paul met with the church (verse 26) for a year and taught great numbers of people. From this we can see that discipling is not merely about conversion and encouraging young Christians to share their faith with others. We all meet to be instructed in the word of God and the fact that they stayed in Antioch a year doing this, shows that it is not a quick process, something you pick up in an odd half-hour. It is a regular process of systematic study, in which you expose your thinking and your behaviour to God's truth. God wants it that way and so do awakened people. Solid biblical teaching is essential for the growth and development of the church.

The other two examples of church growth can be examined more briefly. In Acts 17, we see described the church in Thessalonica. Here the first outreach is not to interested Gentiles, but to a Jewish synagogue:

> When they [Paul and Silas] had passed through Amphipolis and Apollonia, they came to Thessalonica, where there was a Jewish synagogue. As his custom was, Paul went into the synagogue, and on three Sabbath days he reasoned with them from the Scriptures, explaining and proving that the Christ had to suffer and rise from the dead. 'This Jesus I am proclaiming to you is the Christ,' he said. Some of the Jews were persuaded and joined Paul and Silas, as did a large number of God-fearing Greeks and not a few prominent women (Acts 17:1-4).

As before, these were people who were already in the orbit of the synagogue, people who knew something about God and his word. One of the interesting features in Acts is that, although the needs and content of the message never change, the early Church clearly suited its approach to the situation of the people they were trying to reach. We should not expect to be able to reach everybody equally effectively. But here was a group of 'church goers', people who heard the Old Testament read every Sabbath day, people who believed in the one God, but who had not yet come to a real personal knowledge of Jesus for themselves. Perhaps that is the position of some of you who are reading this. Maybe you go to church, but you are not really a Christian yet. Paul and Silas spent three weeks there and taught them that the mission of the Messiah (about whom these people already knew from the Old Testament) had been fulfilled. He had suffered and risen from the dead. And they revealed the identity of the Messiah—Jesus was the Christ. They preached the person and the work of Christ; who Jesus was and what he had done. It is the same good news whether delivered in Antioch or Thessalonica, but here the message is given in a different way to people from another background.

Look at the verbs in verses 2 and 3. Paul reasoned with them from the scriptures, explaining and proving; this approach should be part of our own evangelism too. Both Paul and the Jews were firmly grounded in Scripture. It was their common authority, which naturally Paul took and used. You can imagine him building on the Messianic Psalms or the Servant songs of Isaiah. He dialogued with them. This implies that there were frequent discussions and explanations of what Christians believe, with the scriptural evidence and proof, so that the reasonability of the faith was presented.

This provides a valuable corrective to some contemporary approaches to people who are already religiously inclined. I know, of course, that nobody becomes a Christian by reasoning alone, but neither can anyone be a real Christian if his mind is not convinced of the truth. A merely emotional response is no response at all. We must beware of people being emotionally manipulated to respond to what we might think is Christian truth. You see, there can be common, human emotional experiences, in which the predominant ingredients are not necessarily spiritual at all. They may be perfectly good and valid, but the fact that they are in a Christian context does not make them spiritually authentic, in a truly Christian sense.

Let me illustrate. Some evangelistic rallies are almost indistinguishable in form from secular pop concerts. The music is similar and the response of the audience to the band performing is identical, in terms of their participation. The only difference is that the words are 'Christian' though sometimes even they are ambiguous or inaudible. If people are encouraged to 'respond to Christ' in such a context we surely owe it to them to make sure that they are not simply on an emotional high induced by a powerful beat or crowd hysteria. That is not what New Testament evangelism was about. Paul's gospel had solid biblical content and we need never be afraid of that. We must reason and explain and prove. We are not to be in the business of trying to get people to relax and switch off, as if we could quickly sweep them by emotion into the kingdom of God.

Paul was not being 'intellectual' in the wrong sense. You can present the gospel in a coldly analytical way that makes no difference to anyone, but that is not what is described here, because clearly in this passage Paul appealed to the will. The verb in verse 4 is 'persuaded': persuaded by the truth of what they heard to act upon it, with the result that they joined Paul and Silas. It was not, therefore, an emotional response alone, because it also affected their wills. They broke with their synagogue worship, became Christians, and the church in Thessalonica was born. The new group could never have existed within the synagogue as a party or a faction. It was a totally new entity, one that provoked furious opposition; this is what successful evangelism often does. The Jews stirred up some bad characters from the market place, formed a mob and started a riot in the city.

Lastly, we can study the church in Ephesus, recorded in Acts 19:

> Paul entered the synagogue and spoke boldly there for three months, arguing persuasively about the kingdom of God. But some of them became obstinate; they refused to believe and publicly maligned the Way. So Paul left them. He took the disciples with him and had discussions daily in the lecture hall of Tyrannus. This went on for two years, so that all the Jews and Greeks who lived in the province of Asia heard the word of the Lord. God did extraordinary miracles through Paul. Handkerchiefs and aprons that had touched him were taken to the sick and their illnesses were cured and the evil spirits left them (Acts 19:8-12).

Then we read of how opposition and those who tried to emulate Paul were stirred up by Satan:

> When this [that is, the power of the Lord] became known to the Jews and Greeks living in Ephesus, they were all seized with fear, and the name of the Lord Jesus was held in high honour. Many of those who believed now came and openly confessed their evil deeds. A number who had practised sorcery brought their scrolls together and burned them publicly. When they calculated the value of the scrolls, the total came to fifty thousand drachmas [a drachma is a day's wage]. In this way the word of the Lord spread widely and grew in power (Acts 19:17-20).

This third example is a church that was formed from an essentially pagan community, but also from interested Gentiles and a Jewish synagogue. Here, as everywhere, Paul begins with the God-fearers. But he seems, from verse 8, not to have been very successful in the synagogue. And so he moved on. There was nothing wrong with his message—he preached the kingdom of God—or with his method, since he spoke boldly and argued persuasively; but he ran into an obstinate hardness of heart. They refused to believe and publicly maligned the Way. He gave them three months, and then was asked to leave in any case. So he departed, taking with him those who were disciples. But then he moved on to neutral ground.

It is noticeable that while he was operating in the synagogue, there is no indication that any pagans were actually converted. It was not until he moved on to neutral ground that he made any impact on the pagan community. Like Jesus before him, when Paul met with stubborn refusal he went elsewhere. So he hired a lecture hall, belonging to Tyrannus. The Western Text of the New Testament adds that he hired it from the hours of 11.00 a.m. to 4.00 p.m.—siesta time. Tyrannus was teaching his philosophy up to 11.00 and probably collecting a handsome fee for it. Paul conducted his extra-mural classes until 4.00 when people had some free time to come and listen, but after the main heat of the day was over. He had these discussions daily, for as long as two years. Again, this policy of patient sowing and long-term nurturing of evangelistic contacts is very different from our modern patterns. Paul was apparently prepared to spend time in clearing away objections, listening to difficulties and showing his hearers the logical consistency of his message. In contrast, we are often so keen to get on to the next group, or to cover more ground, that we are content to spray a wide area with a dilute solution of the gospel, or to indulge in 'hit and run' evangelism, as it is sometimes called.

In trying to deal with people who have no Christian background, we need to look for equivalents of that neutral ground. Many non-Christians are reluctant about coming to a church building, if not actually intimidated. It is a severe culture-shock as far as they are concerned. We have to learn to build bridges to them and to approach them on their own ground, in ways and locations with which they feel comfortable. When Paul hired the lecture hall of Tyrannus and held his discussions, there were enough people coming to make it worthwhile for two years. Indeed we read in verse 10 that all the Jews and Greeks who lived in the province of Asia heard the word of the Lord, which means that there was total penetration of that area with the truth of God.

Furthermore, in a pagan society with no knowledge of God, God performed some extraordinary miracles (verse 11). This does not mean that God always did miracles like that, even in the days of the New Testament church. Luke says they are extraordinary, by anybody's standards, but in Ephesus God did them. And God can still perform extraordinary miracles whenever he chooses to. We should not limit the sovereignty and the authority of God. He can do anything he chooses, to authenticate his word. Verses 13-19 show us the kind of environment in which

Paul was operating. In Ephesus there were exorcists, clair-voyants, sorcerers, magicians and all sorts of occult prac-tices, and God, in his infinite mercy, stoops to lost people like that, to rescue them by demonstrating that his power in the supernatural realm is utterly superior.

So we see many different approaches: preaching, discus-sion, sharing, reasoning and proving, and then God chooses in his sovereignty to do something extraordinary among these superstitious people, in order that there may be a real breakthrough for the gospel. In our culture we can similarly trust God to demonstrate his power in sup-port of his word. But it is not through miracles alone that people are converted as John's gospel so clearly states. Even after Jesus had done all his miraculous signs the people would still not believe in him (Jn 12:37). It is the truth of the message that the Holy Spirit brings home to the mind and heart by which people's lives are changed. And we see from Acts 19:18 that the secret disciples came out into the open and, along with the converted disciples of Apollos who we meet at the beginning of the chapter, the Ephesian church was founded.

Furthermore, we see in verse 20 that it was growing: 'In this way the word of the Lord spread widely and grew in power.' It had a long way to go out of paganism, but it was moving forward from the very start. It is vital, at this point, to notice that the *word* is the agent by which it happened, not Paul, not techniques, but God's truth. In the original Greek the words for 'spread' and 'grew' are in the imperfect tense, which means that it kept on happening, and it still does. Our business is growing. But only God gives the increase, and he does it as we learn and follow his principles of growth. We have to become available channels for his truth, those who are ready and willing to talk about Jesus. People whose confidence is in the word and in the Spirit are people who expect great things from a great God.

3

Motives and Methods in Evangelism

I wonder if you sometimes imagine that the apostle Paul was a 'super hero' Christian, who had no problems at all in fulfilling Christ's commission to his people, to be his witnesses and declare the good news of Jesus with the whole world. So often for us Christians, in the twentieth century, evangelism seems so difficult. Evangelism, of course, simply means telling good news. But it seems for us a hard thing to do, a duty to be carried out rather than a privilege and, if we are honest, many of us have something of a guilty conscience about it. The awareness hangs over us that we really ought to be doing more, but somehow we cannot manage it and we do not live up to what we would like to be. As a result, we find the growth in the early church, of the sort we have been studying, somewhat daunting, not to say threatening. Instead of being excited by the possibility of expansion, we tend to dig our trench a little bit deeper. We rightly realize that church growth depends largely on one-to-one communication, but we hesitate to become too involved in that because it sounds a dangerous business and it can be lonely out there in the big wide world.

The passage we are going to examine in this chapter,

1 Thessalonians 2:1-9, is tremendously exciting because it shows us Paul sharing honestly with Christians in Thessalonica the problems that he had faced, when first he came to their city. These included both opposition from other people and also the problems of his own inner attitudes and motives. The encouraging thing is that Paul, the great apostle, was not so different from us; but even more, he is able to show us a way through the problems, which is just what we need. If you visit Hampton Court and get lost in the maze, you really have no idea where you are or how to get out. At first, it is enormous fun; but if someone comes along after a little while and you say, 'I seem to be lost,' and they reply, 'So am I,' and the next person says the same and the next, the fun seems to evaporate. Sympathy is marvellous for five minutes; 'Here we are, all in the same boat! Never mind! It will all work out all right.' Of course, if it is the Hampton Court maze, it will work out all right, because they will get you out by the end of the day: but it is no good just having someone to sit down and say, 'Yes, I know what it feels like.' You want to find the way out. And it is no good somebody coming along and saying, 'Yes, I have a problem in evangelism too.' We want to find the way through.

Here, Paul gives us some very practical and helpful ways by which to achieve the purposes God has for us.

You know, brothers, that our visit to you was not a failure. We had previously suffered and been insulted in Philippi, as you know, but with the help of our God we dared to tell you his gospel in spite of strong opposition. For the appeal we make does not spring from error or impure motives, nor are we trying to trick you. On the contrary, we speak as men approved by God to be entrusted with the gospel. We are not trying to please men but God, who tests our hearts. You know we never used flattery, nor did we put on a mask to cover up greed—God is our witness. We were not looking for praise from men, not from you or anyone else. As apostles of

Christ we could have been a burden to you, but we were gentle among you, like a mother caring for her little children. We loved you so much that we were delighted to share with you not only the gospel of God but our lives as well, because you had become so dear to us. Surely you remember, brothers, our toil and hardship; we worked night and day in order not to be a burden to anyone while we preached the gospel of God to you (1 Thess 2:1-9).

The passage divides into two. Verses 1-6 deal with the temptations Paul faced and overcame. They are concerned with the area of his motives and how he managed to get on with the job of sharing the good news with other people. Verses 7-9 refer to the methods he used and why his work was so greatly owned by God. I hope they will encourage us to realize that God has not called us to an impossible task called evangelism. He simply invites us to prove his promises and his power, by being available to share both the gospel and our own selves with other people.

The first temptation Paul faced and overcame, recorded in verses 1 and 2, was that of apathy or inactivity, the temptation not to bother. Many of us can identify with that, I am sure. When the subject of evangelism comes up the talk is about sharing the good news with other people. We prefer to pass; we would rather not bother. But have you ever asked yourself why? Basically, many Christians are afraid. We are frightened, firstly, of failure. Paul tells them, 'You know, brothers, that our visit to you was not a failure' (verse 1). But we are also frightened by the sort of opposition that the end of verse 2 talks about—'*strong* opposition'. The temptation not to bother was something that Paul faced when he arrived in Thessalonica. After all, he had just been imprisoned, beaten and put in the stocks at Philippi, only about a hundred miles away. Although he and Silas had been able to sing hymns at midnight and although there had been an earthquake and the jailer had become a Christian, let us not imagine that Paul was a super hero who did not feel these things. The experience must surely have hurt him. His body was bruised, black and blue. He was hurt emotionally and psychologically. All the time, as he went on his missionary journeys, there were people who were trying to undermine his work, especially those who were devoted to the Jewish synagogues. We know from the New Testament letters the sneering insinuations that they spread about him—an unbalanced fanatic, a hopeless extremist. Other people were only too ready to accuse Paul of preaching for only selfish reasons: 'He wants to exploit gullible people, in order to feather his own nest. His preaching is just an extended ego trip.' Make no mistake—it hurt.

I have no doubt that as he arrived in Thessalonica there was that voice within saying, 'Why do you bother, Paul? You may fail again. You may run into all sorts of tough opposition. It's going to be dangerous, Paul. Why not give it a miss?' The temptation not to bother is so often the devil's first method. And when, after three weeks, he had to run, to leave the city by night, because of the opposition that was after his life and to go all the way down to Corinth in the deep south, do you not think that as he went that same voice was saying, 'It didn't work, did it Paul? The opposition was too strong. Why go on? You could have a very comfortable, prestigious teaching position in a Hebrew university, somewhere. Why don't you settle down?' Christians who are at all involved in evangelism recognize that tape, playing in their minds. 'You muffed it at work last time, didn't you? Why bother again? You know how she cooled towards you when you mentioned the name of Christ. Don't say it again when she's there, will you? They'll just hit the roof at home if you witness to them, so just forget it. Why bother?' That is the giant fear which paralyses so many Christian people—fear of failure and fear of the opposition, both of which tempt us not to bother. But how do you get out of that sort of maze?

Look at verse 2. 'We had previously suffered and been insulted in Philippi, as you know, but with the help of our God we dared to tell you his gospel in spite of strong opposition.' Literally, the phrase 'with the help of our God' means 'we grew bold in our God'. In other words, Paul is saying that God himself was the source of the courage he had to preach to them in spite of all that he had suffered and all his fears. Paul had grasped this fantastic truth that the gospel he proclaimed was the gospel of God. Several times in this letter he states that. But particularly in verse 2 he describes it as '*his* [God's] gospel,' and again at the end of verse 9 'the gospel of God'. That is why the gospel is going to succeed. God is committed to it and, in a sense, God takes the responsibility for it. The messenger does not have to carry that load. His task is to be faithful and tell the gospel as it is.

It is very liberating to realize that it is not ultimately up to us to be 'successful'. We do not have to send in our returns to God, as it were, and say, 'This is what I have achieved in my evangelism.' If we operate that way, people will not be able to see Christ; they will just see us. We need to have confidence that the gospel is not going to fail, because God is committed to the truth. So often, we are afraid that if we do not *see* the gospel at work nothing is happening. But you can only see the tip of an iceberg. So we are not to judge what God is doing by limited impressions of what that is. Our privilege is to be a link in his chain. We only have to be available, for God to use us, in the strength of his Spirit. We do not therefore have to fear failure because wherever we say a word for Christ, wherever Christ's love flows through us, wherever Jesus is seen in our lives, the good news is being communicated. God makes it count, to the end of extending his kingly rule in human lives. He can use a telephone call, a letter that you write, a booklet you may send to someone, a casual conversation, an act of kindness, a prayer. If you are prepared to be available, you can be a link in God's chain, by which he is committed to drawing a multitude of people to himself. Heaven is not going to be unpopulated. It will be full of people brought from all over the world to acknowledge him as Lord, because there have been Christians who have been prepared to be available as Christ's messengers and to trust him to work through them, by his almighty power.

The second great temptation that Paul faced, in verses 3–6, was the temptation to compromise. 'For the appeal we make does not spring from error' (verse 3a). There are those who have decided to change the content of the Christian message in order to make it, as they think, more palatable to those who are not yet Christians. That is a serious mistake. The word translated 'error' here, literally means 'wandering from the right path'. Paul did not call these Thessalonians to faith in a merely human Jesus, though that is what some want to do today. Their message is that Jesus was a great man, so why don't you follow him? But that is not the gospel. Others preach that Jesus is a great example, so why don't you try to live your life the Jesus way? But again, that is not the gospel, as anyone who seriously tries to live that way will soon discover. Paul preached Jesus as a Saviour, who rescues people who know they cannot help themselves. He would never compromise that essential.

Nor did Paul soft-peddle man's sin and God's judgement. The apostolic preaching of the gospel did not promise, 'If you come to Christ, all your problems will be solved.' They will not be. When a person becomes a Christian, he or she exchanges the problems of a non-Christian for those of a Christian. The difference, however, is that they now have an unchanging eternal friend with whom to share them, and the resource of divine power with which to cope with them. But our problems are not all solved immediately, because we are human and we live in a world that is fallen and broken. Paul did not preach that Christ would top you up in those areas of life where you are lacking, and then you will live happily ever after. Again, that is not the gospel. Christians suffer and go through the mill. We all experience many sorts of pressures. He did not subtly change the gospel to try to get people to believe it. He spoke of repentance; he spoke of serving the Lord God; he spoke of the cost of being committed as a Christian—you find this in 1 Thessalonians 1:9, 10 where he summarizes the message upon which the Thessalonian church was founded: 'you turned to God from idols to serve the living and true God, and to wait for his Son from heaven, whom he raised from the dead— Jesus, who rescues us from the coming wrath.'

'On the contrary,' Paul says, 'we speak as men approved by God to be entrusted with the gospel' (1 Thess 2:4). However much his message was opposed, Paul never forgot that God has chosen him to be his witness. Similarly, we have been appointed to the same service by the same king who in his commission has given us the same message, which we are not at liberty to change by one word. It is not negotiable.

The good news is that the universal creator and ruler proclaims peace to men, but does so on his own terms. These are that men lay down their arms and stop fighting him; that they repent of their sins; that they trust their lives to him; and that they obey him. The gospel is a call to submit to God and to follow him. All that is possible because Christ died that we might be forgiven and because he rose again to give his eternal life, here and now, in the personalities of all who turn from sin and trust in him. That is the gospel. And it is true of churches, as well as individuals, that if we do not proclaim that message, we shall neither know God's blessing, nor see any lasting fruit. Paul defeated the temptation to compromise the content of the gospel by realizing that he had to stand one day before the God who had called him, to give an account of his stewardship. Because he had been approved by God and entrusted with the gospel, he would not change one word of it.

Secondly, he faced the temptation to compromise in *why* he was saying it. He states in verse 3, 'The appeal we make does not spring from error or *impure* motives.' What that means is best explained by his further statement in verse 5: 'You know we never used flattery, nor did we put on a mask to cover up greed—God is our witness.' The facts clearly spoke for themselves, that Paul had overcome any temptations that he may have had to motives that were less than Christian. Flattery is telling people what they want to hear so that they will do what you want them to do. If you are involved in telling people about Christ, that can sometimes be a temptation. Paul also put on one side 'a mask for greed'. Such a mask disguises the fact that you are out for your own ends, by pretending to be concerned with the person who you are in fact exploiting. Either of those motives is sub-Christian.

For Paul, this probably meant he would not accept payment for his preaching. There were plenty of smooth-talking charlatans around in Paul's day. New cults and philosophies were two a penny and they were designed to fleece the unsuspecting and to line the pockets of those who propagated them. Paul would have nothing to do with that. It is true that today you are not likely to become a millionaire by being an evangelist, which is probably just as well! But we face equivalent temptations in other ways. There is the sort of evangelistic approach that does not tell people the whole story until they have committed themselves. There is a kind of evangelism that seems to prey on defenceless people, playing on their emotions, where the evangelist appears to be more concerned about the numbers of people who respond and about his own success or status, than about the people to whom he is communicating and their ultimate spiritual well-being. We have all of us met situations like that.

I remember a boy years ago, in an evangelistic coffee bar, saying to me, 'All these Christians here are telling me that they love me. Now, do they love me because they want to convert me, or do they want to convert me because they love me?' He had seen through the superficiality of what sometimes passes as evangelism. What was coming across to him was a concern for a statistic rather than for him as an individual. There can be an attitude of netting people, or even scalp hunting, which is unworthy of the name of Jesus. That boy had every right to ask for real proof of the love which those Christians professed towards him. We all know the temptation to get quick results by flattery, or by disguising what we are saying, but what problems those methods create and how they weaken and divert the church from its task of making real disciples.

The final area of temptation was in *how* they communicated the message. Paul identifies this at the end of verse 3; 'Nor are we trying to trick you.' He affirms that his method was not a crafty, scheming approach. One of the saddest experiences I have ever had, in a Christian meeting, was being subjected to a very long process of what the gentleman who was leading the meeting was pleased to call 'softening up', during which a great deal of music and singing occurred. At the end of this lengthy process, we were told, 'Now you are ready!' With a big smile on his face, the leader told us, 'After that you'll believe anything I tell you.' It is hard to imagine a more sub-Christian device than that. The Christian gospel does not have to be promoted by drugging people, or by getting them to switch off their minds, in order to carry them along on an emotional tide. The biblical gospel can stand up to the most rigorous intellectual analysis anybody likes to apply, because it is the truth. We do not have to stoop to the compromise of trying to trick or manoeuvre people. We must, with Paul, resolve to have nothing to do with such underhanded ways.

Paul's way through the maze was to realize that what other people thought of him, however hurtful, was irrelevant in the last analysis. Look at the two statements at the end of verse 4 and the beginning of verse 6: 'We are not trying to please men but God, who tests our hearts . . . We are not looking for praise from men, not from you or anyone else.' If our Christian service is motivated by wanting other people to be pleased with us, then it is not Christian service at all. That can be a terrible snare, but such judgements are ultimately irrelevant. It is what God sees when he tests our hearts that matters. If we live our lives before him, that will take us out of the temptation to compromise by playing to the gallery. We are not living for the crowd; we are serving the Lord. When we are tempted to compromise our message, our motives or our method, we must remember that the gospel is the truth and that we are serving the living God, not men.

The remaining verses, 7–9, take us to the positive principles that Paul adopted. Let me suggest that there are three, one in each of the verses. They all refer to Paul's own attitude as he served God in Thessalonica. In verse 7, he says that he and Silas were not a burden, but gentle; in verse 8, not remote, but sharing; and in verse 9, not demanding, but hard-working. These principles well repay a little closer examination. 'As apostles of Christ we could have been a burden [literally, a 'heaviness'] to you, but we were gentle among you, like a mother caring for her little children' (verse 7). This shows us that when Paul first came among them, he was not full of himself and his office as an apostle. He did not begin by presenting his own apostolic credentials, because he was not weighty with his own importance. He did not pull rank. He was so full of Jesus Christ that people were drawn to the Lord, not his servant. When you met Paul, he was a friendly person, easy to talk to, caring and sensitive in the way he dealt with other people. We know from his letters that he could be very firm; but even then there was a gentleness in his firmness that mirrored a mother's care. What more loving, gentle picture could you have than a mother nursing and cherishing her children?

That is what God calls us to be, as we share the gospel. Not heavy, like a dumper-truck unloading its contents onto other people, but gentle and caring, as a mother is for her children. That is not weakness. It is the strength of a love that is unbreakable. If we want to help people to Christ and to see our churches grow, then we must be channels of Christ's love to them. We can do so much harm by force-feeding truth down unwilling throats. But Paul was not like that. Rather, his gentleness continued after they had become Christians, because now they were Paul's spiritual children and he naturally felt a strong bond of spiritual affection, as well as responsibility, for them. I know there is a place for challenge and a place for straight talk, but it must always be in love. There is a gentleness that wins people, which we would do well to ask God to give us, in emulation of Paul.

In verse 8, Paul tells us he was not remote, but sharing: 'We loved you so much that we were delighted to share with you not only the gospel of God but our lives as well, because you had become so dear to us.' Isn't that a marvellous statement? It shows us that evangelism for Paul was not a series of 'hit and run raids'. It was not a matter of creeping down the garden path with a tract, slipping it through the door and nipping off again before they see me. It would never have occurred to him to behave like that, because he loved people too much. We do that either because we are scared or because we do not have time for individuals. I know from experience how demanding it is to knock on a door, when you have no idea what the response will be. But if we are going to love people for Christ's sake, the least we can do is talk with them. More remote methods may have a place, but usually it is only because the basic New Testament method is not being used. The primary method in the New Testament is loving friendship that shares, not only the gospel but our own selves as well.

It is the same principle as the mother in verse 7 adapting to the needs of her child. She loves that baby, so she does all she can to nurture and cherish the child. It is a love prepared to share everything we have that wins people to Jesus. If we do not love people, let us not try to witness to them. First, let us get down on our knees to God and implore him to forgive and to melt our hard hearts until we begin to see people as Jesus sees them, until we begin to overflow with his love and can say, with Paul, that our greatest joy is to share the gospel of God. But we are not going to be sharing it like spraying insecticide on roses, at arm's length! It involves sharing our own lives as well. That is both the cost of effective evangelism and its joy. You cannot give the message without giving the messenger. That's the Jesus way!

This point was memorably illustrated for me in the story of a Japanese Christian girl whom I once heard telling how she became a follower of Jesus. She had come to this country to study at a university, not knowing anything at all about the Christian faith. In her hall of residence, she was allotted a room next door to a Christian, who began to befriend her in a most natural, relaxed way. The Christian girl showed her Japanese friend around the campus, helped her to fit into life in this rather different culture, and did all she could to make her stay here enjoyable. They were frequently in one another's rooms drinking coffee, and on one evening the Japanese girl asked the Christian what the book beside her bed was.

She replied that it was a Bible and invited the Japanese girl to spend time for just a few minutes each evening reading the Bible with her. After a period of months, meeting other Christians, reading Christian books and generally examining the claims of Christ, the Japanese girl came to trust in Jesus for herself. There had been many links in the chain, but the most important was the time that the Christian girl was prepared to spend in sharing her own life with the girl from Japan, as well as the gospel of Christ. I shall never forget the smile on the Japanese girl's face as she told us, 'You see, my English friend built that bridge of friendship into my heart, and over the bridge walked Jesus.' If we want to be remote from people, we have got the wrong religion. Christianity is not a religion of distance. Christians are to wash people's feet, to go the second mile, above all to love and care. That can only be done by getting involved.

Lastly, in verse 9, Paul says he was not demanding but hard-working: 'Surely you remember, brothers, our toil and hardship; we worked night and day in order not to be a burden to anyone while we preached the gospel of God to you.' Paul was a Rabbi initially, and all rabbis had a trade. He was prepared to work hard at his, which was tentmaking, supporting himself, so that as much of his time as possible could be devoted to the gospel. He tells us in 1 Corinthians 9 that he had the right to be supported as an apostle, as the others were, but in his case he waived that right, so as to be free to proclaim the gospel, without anybody being able to say that they had paid him, or he had made a good living out of it. It was this passion that governed his life. He demonstrated that he was not a burden to people, but a blessing; never demanding, but hardworking.

From a different angle, that same principle is very important for us as we share the gospel. If other people at work or at home have to work harder because we do not pull our weight, and they know that we are Christians, what are they going to think about Jesus Christ? If we continually sew up other Christians' time, burdening them with our problems, when we should be working hard for the Lord, what does that say about our concern for God's lost world. Of course, we all need to share our problems from time to time, but I am concerned at how easy it is for Christians to become drones in God's hive instead of busy bees. Sadly, there are Christians who just drone on and burden everyone in sight with their difficulties and problems, when if they would only be prepared to get up and do something for someone else, they would find the help that begins to lift the problems, because once you start giving, you receive from God. Paul was not demanding of others. He was hard-working, so that the gospel might spread.

These are the methods that count if the church is to grow—gentleness, sharing not just the message but our own lives, working hard so that we are not a burden on anyone, in order that the gospel may speed on and triumph (2 Thess 3:1). It is very significant that the great missionary apostle does not give us a catalogue of techniques. What he gives us is a character towards which we are to progress, because in the end, what we are shouts louder than what we say.

4

Establishing Priorities

Now we focus our lens on that prototype church in Jerusalem, to see what we can learn from the first spirit-filled community of at least 3,120 Christians. As we study these verses at the end of Acts 2, I know that God will challenge us regarding our own priorities today. That was in fact the first challenge the apostles themselves faced. They had to establish under God certain priorities for the Christians. We can see, with hindsight, even if they were unaware at the time, that those priorities were crucial for the spread of the gospel. It is a continuing challenge in every generation to all Christians, including ourselves.

The reason is not far to seek. We are finite, and we have only limited time, energy and resources. This means that each of us faces the question practically in our lives as a member of the church of Jesus Christ, of what we are going to major on, in what we are going to invest time and talents.

When the people heard this [Peter's sermon and declaration that Jesus is Lord and Christ], they were cut to the heart and said to Peter and the other apostles, 'Brothers, what shall we do?' Peter replied, 'Repent and be baptised every one of you, in the name of Jesus Christ so that your sins may be forgiven.

57

And you will receive the gift of the Holy Spirit. The promise
is for you and your children and for all who are far off—for all
whom the Lord our God will call.' With many other words
he warned them; and he pleaded with them, 'Save yourselves
from this corrupt generation.' Those who accepted his
message were baptised, and about three thousand were added
to their number that day. They devoted themselves to the
apostles' teaching and to the fellowship, to the breaking of
bread and to prayer. Everyone was filled with awe, and many
wonders and miraculous signs were done by the apostles. All
the believers were together and had everything in common.
Selling their possessions and goods, they gave to anyone as he
had need. Every day they continued to meet together in the
temple courts. They broke bread in their homes and ate
together with glad and sincere hearts, praising God and
enjoying the favour of all the people. And the Lord added to
their number daily those who were being saved (Acts 2:37-
47).

What should be our practical priorities? That question is
answered at the heart of this passage in Acts 2: 42: 'They
devoted themselves to the apostles' teaching and to the
fellowship, to the breaking of bread and to prayer.' If you
wanted to write a modern paraphrase, you would put the
first verb in that verse as something like 'they were dead
keen' on these things. This was what obsessed them. Here
were their priorities. From them we can find continuing
principles for the church, for Christians in every generation.

Before we look at those ingredients, notice how this
church came to be in existence. Verse 37: 'When the people
heard [Peter's sermon], they were cut to the heart and said
to Peter and the other apostles, "Brothers, what shall we
do?"' The church in Jerusalem was brought about by the
preaching of Peter in the power of the Spirit. They heard
the word that Peter spoke and were cut to their hearts.
That is, the Holy Spirit took the word that Peter preached

and applied it with such authority and conviction that they could not be the same people afterwards. If you pray for the ministry on Sunday in your church, you should remember that priority. Too often in the contemporary church we hear the word, go home and roast the preacher for lunch, or else write it in our notebook and say it was quite an interesting address. How much do we need the power of the Spirit to communicate and receive God's dynamic truth in a life-changing way!

Peter's preaching was all about Christ. The sermon effectively begins (verse 22) where he says, 'Men of Israel, listen to this: Jesus . . .' Jesus is the first word of his sermon and Jesus is the focus of everything he says. He tells them that Jesus was a man, so beginning with the historical reality of Christ's existence. Christianity is no mere theory—it is grounded in the factual reality of a life that was really lived, in time and space, in our world. Having reminded his hearers of the way in which God confirmed the identity of Jesus through his miracles, Peter moved on to talk about his death (verse 23): 'This man was handed over to you by God's set purpose and foreknowledge; and you, with the help of wicked men, put him to death by nailing him to the cross.' The death of Jesus is attributed both to the sinfulness of man and the saving purposes of God. Then he moves on to the resurrection in verse 24: 'But God raised him from the dead.' It is important to remember Peter's sermon as we see it here in note form. No one knows how long the actual sermon took but clearly it was longer than the two minutes it takes us to read this summary.

After dealing with Christ's person, death and resurrection, Peter quotes from Psalm 16 in the Old Testament, relating how all this had been foretold by God: 'you will not abandon me to the grave, nor will you let your Holy One see decay.' This Old Testament teaching, says Peter, has been fulfilled (verse 32). God had raised this Jesus to life and the apostles were the living witnesses of that reality. Then in verse 33 he describes the ascension and exultation of Christ, which confirms that he is the Son of God, now seated at the Father's right hand. Furthermore, Christ had now sent the Holy Spirit upon the church, in fulfilment of his promise. It is a masterpiece of clear evangelistic preaching. Peter takes Old Testament scripture, then New Testament fact, joins the two together and proclaims them as the word of God. The Holy Spirit takes that word about who Jesus is and what he has done—the gospel—and applies it to the hearts of those who hear, with the result that they cry out, 'What shall we do?' The word plus the Spirit makes the church. The people who heard a full declaration of Christ's person made a full response to him (verse 38): 'Repent and be baptised . . . so that your sins may be forgiven.'

There cannot be a church unless there is a preaching of the truth, unless the Holy Spirit works in people's lives and unless there is a response in those who are the believers, first of all of repentance. This entails a change of mind about Christ, about our attitude to him and a subsequent change of direction in our lives. That in turn involves us turning to him as Saviour and Lord, not secretly but openly, being baptized and living our lives for him, rather than ourselves. Thus, verse 41 tells us that those who had accepted his message were baptized and about 3,000 were added to their number that day. There was an inner response of faith and repentance towards the Lord Jesus, which was marked by the outward visible sign of baptism. The baptism of believers in Jesus, particularly by immersion, is still a graphic portrayal of the death and burial of our old self-centred way of living and of our resurrection with Christ to a new life, in the power of the Holy Spirit. These are the responses that make the church.

Nor was it just the Jerusalem church, because verse 39 shows that the same pattern is true in every generation:

'The promise is for you and your children and all who are far off—for all whom the Lord our God will call.' The gifts of forgiveness and of the Holy Spirit are not for some elitist group within the church. The promise of the gift is for *all* who repent and who believe the good news. Both the forgiveness of sins and the receiving of the Spirit are blessings of salvation that you acquire when you first respond to the call of God. Without them you cannot be a member of the church of Christ. That is the first priority to establish. The church is made up of people who have been forgiven through the death of Jesus, because they have repented of their sins and who, in that, have received the life of Jesus, through the gift of the Holy Spirit. His purpose within Christians is to change our lives and to make us the new people of God.

Notice that here there is no record of wind and fire or foreign languages, though that accompanied the filling of the disciples at the beginning of the chapter on the day of Pentecost. For the 3,000 we are not told specifically that they received tongues of fire or that they spoke in unknown tongues themselves. It simply says that here was a company of born-again people who knew that they had been forgiven and who had the life of Christ within them. And *that* is the New Testament definition of the church. It is, therefore, a personal priority for every one of us to ask ourselves if we really belong to the universal church of Christ. Have we repented? Have we believed? Is the Holy Spirit within us? These are the evidences of God's work in our lives. Now if that is true of us, then the evidence will not just be looking back to a past experience when these things occurred. The real evidence is that we share the priorities of Christ today.

To what is it that Spirit-filled Christians should be devoting themselves? The first priority is in instruction: 'They devoted themselves to the apostles' teaching.' This church put learning and practising the truth at the top of their list. The apostles did not revel in a mystical experience that despises the intellect and puts teaching to one side. Nor could the infant church dispense with human teachers because they now had the Holy Spirit. They gave themselves to the teaching of the apostles and as they did that, they submitted to the apostolic authority which verse 43 tells us God confirmed and authenticated by miracles.

It is very important to grasp this because there is a crisis of authority in evangelical churches today. People are asking how we can know what God's teaching is. How do we know what he is saying in our situation today? Clearly it is a very important question to ask. For example, we have people who claim to be latter-day apostles who are vehicles for the word of God today. We have to ask, if that is so, does their teaching have the same divine authority as that of the New Testament writers? Should we look for miracles to confirm the office of apostles in the 1980s as they did apparently on the day of Pentecost? To answer this, we need a biblical doctrine of miracles.

It is so easy for Christians to gravitate between positions. On the one hand, there are some Christians who almost deny that any miracles could be done today. That is a patently false position because, within the consistency of his character, God is a free agent. He is sovereign and does what he wills; his power is no less today than it was on the day of Pentecost. But at the other end of the spectrum, it is equally unbalanced to expect miracles today with the same frequency as they occurred in the life of Jesus, or in the earliest experience of the church. Even the apostles did not do greater works than Jesus did in the sense that is often claimed. They did not turn water into wine, feed 5,000 from one boy's lunch, or walk on water. They were sometimes able to heal and occasionally even to raise the dead, but these were notable, rather than everyday occurrences, and they were not in themselves greater works than Jesus did.

This leads me to believe that it was spiritual miracles of new birth on a much larger scale than had ever been seen in the ministry of Jesus to which he was referring when he promised his disciples that they would do even greater things (Jn 14:12). Today, no one is doing physical miracles in quite the way he did. If they were, I suggest you would not be able to get near them for the crowds. It is also a wrong understanding of the Bible to think that miracles are sprinkled all the way through its pages, as it were indiscriminately. That is not so. If you investigate the biblical pattern of miracles, you will see that they do not occur with equal regularity all the way through Scripture, but they are, by definition, exceptions to the normal. If they were normal, they would not be miracles. They occur in clusters. As you look through the Bible at its miracles, you will find that they focus at special times, when God is unveiling a new stage in his progressive self-revelation.

For example, in the Old Testament, miracles were performed through Moses at the time when the people of God came out of Egypt and were being led through the wilderness, which is also when God was revealing his truth in the law. He authenticated his revelation through these miracles. Similarly, later on in the Old Testament, at the time of the beginning of the prophetic ministry, you will find that Elijah and Elisha performed miracles. But most of the other prophets, including all of the later ones, did not have a ministry of miracles. It was through the ministry of the word that God chose to make himself known.

Of course, all this is seen supremely in the Gospels. When the Lord Jesus came into the world, he demonstrated his authority as the Son of God by mighty works and miracles. At the climax of his ministry and vindication, it was by the miracle of the resurrection that God declared Jesus to be his Son, with power (Rom 1:4). Similarly, in

Acts there is another stage of God's revelation, in the founding of the church. The church age begins and at once the gospel penetrates new areas—Jerusalem, Judea, Samaria, to the uttermost parts of the earth—authenticated by miracles. It is highly significant that today, when the gospel penetrates pagan situations and reaches tribes that have never heard of Christ before, the preaching of the good news in those situations may well be authenticated by the miraculous. In that case it is a special sign from God that what is being heard is true, that it is indeed the word of the Lord.

But it was part of the uniqueness of the New Testament apostles that their ministry was vindicated by extraordinary signs and wonders. 2 Corinthians 12:12 speaks about the marks of an apostle—signs, wonders and miracles—which were done among the Corinthian believers. The signs obviously authenticated the apostolic teaching as divine revelation, confirming that the apostles were channels of God's authoritative word.

It is for these reasons that I personally do not think we should expect contemporary equivalents of such events. Of course God's power is unlimited and we can never make rules for what he can or cannot do. We see that power demonstrated in a variety of ways through gifted individuals, in answer to prayer, and we thank God for every demonstration of his sovereign rule of love. But there are no special individuals who are exclusive channels of fresh revelation being authenticated by miraculous signs and wonders today, as the apostles were. This is because we now have the complete Bible, in which God speaks to us fully and finally. We need that word to be explained and applied in our contemporary situation, of course, and God always has more light to give us and more truth to teach us. But it is from his holy word that he does so. He is not giving fresh revelation to men today which could not be found in Scripture.

Because he is the God of both nature and history, it is a distortion to see his self-revelation only in terms of the spectacular and supernatural. He sustains the whole world by his power. We see him in the word, the Bible, every last line, for that where he has chosen to reveal himself authoritatively to his people. What then when someone comes to us today and says, 'I have a word from the Lord for you'? Clearly we need to assess whether or not that is so. Even when acting from the best possible motives we all know how easily we can make mistakes, or be deluded. The only way we can test whether something said is really a word from God is by bringing it to the *authenticated* word of God in the written Scriptures. This is the apostolic teaching in the New Testament, which the Holy Spirit has seen fit to preserve for nearly 2,000 years. Since Scripture is the word of God we can have confidence that what Scripture says, God is saying.

Therefore, anything that anyone brings to you as the word of the Lord today must be tested by Scripture. That must also be a priority of the church. Otherwise, the church will find itself drifting on a tide of relativism where one prophet or another authority can stand up and claim to be speaking from God. The danger in that situation is that the criterion of authority then becomes either the charismatic persona of the speaker or the acceptability of the content. But neither are reliable touchstones. If the person does not testify according to Scripture, there is no guarantee that what is said is a word from God. But if it is in Scripture, if what the person is saying to the church today is clearly there in the Bible, then God is still saying it. One of the purposes of the Holy Spirit living within Christians is to open our minds to understand the Bible. This is not a matter of intellectual ability at all, but of spiritual appetite and desire. There is no clearer evidence of a man being filled with the Spirit than that he should have a great desire to know what the Bible says and to do it.

So then, if someone comes to us, as individuals or to the church, with an idea which they believe God is giving them, our first question must always be, 'What does God say about it in his word?' Not the church tradition, though that can be quite wrongly founded itself. Nor should our prejudices or personal preferences be decisive. Neither reason nor the views of contemporary scholarship should be our infallible guide. No, our main, primary criterion is, 'What does Scripture say?' *That* is the question and that is the number one priority. But it takes hard work to dig that out and to apply it to contemporary issues. It is not all given to us on a plate. 'They devoted themselves to the apostles' teaching.'

Many of us would agree with that. But we need to ask ourselves how much time we actually spend in God's word. To me, one of the saddest facts about much local church life today is that so little time is actually given to the teaching of God's truth. For many, it has been relegated to a ten-minute homily on a Sunday morning, which is often more the preacher's words than God's truth. But it is even sadder to find Christians who are taught God's word and who know what they ought to be doing biblically, not doing it. I suppose that is something every growing Christian has to wrestle with. It is not enough to study Scripture, to acquire doctrinal knowledge and agree with it. The Pharisees had plenty of that. It is the obedience of the heart that matters. These disciples had this teaching from the apostles, not so that they could pass examinations in religious knowledge, but so that their lives could be transformed. Many of us know what to do, but we fail to do it. Many of us are aware of the truth, but we do not practise it. Devoting ourselves to the apostolic teaching does not just mean sagely nodding our heads. It means our wills being exercised and our lives being opened and it means saying to the Lord, 'Lord have mercy on me, a sinner. Make me someone who does your word as well as acknowledging it.' You cannot be a functioning, maturing Christian, without biblical instruction.

The second thing to which they devoted themselves is fellowship. The apostles' teaching and the fellowship are both equally important. You probably know that the word fellowship is *koinonia*, meaning 'to have something in common with somebody else'. It was a word used of shareholders in a company, people who owned a business together like James and John in the 'Zebedee Fishing Company'. As Christians, we participate in a common life. We are shareholders in the life of God, because the risen Lord Jesus has given us his Spirit so that we might live a new quality of life through him. We are all on the same ground before God. That is what fellowship entails. Within a church family and within the whole church around the world, we belong to one another, because we belong to God. There is one Father, and so, as sons and daughters of the living God, share that common life of Christ in his body, because we were made children of God by his grace. It follows that once we have become Christians, each one of us has a unique role to play in that community.

In verse 44, the adjective *koinonikos* appears, which usually means 'generous'. It implies an emphasis on having open hands, on being turned outwards to other people. New Testament fellowship is not you and me together, with our backs turned on the world; but all of us joined together, with open hands and hearts towards one another and towards the world in which God has placed us. The man who prayed, 'Lord, bless me and my wife, my son John and his wife, us four, that's all, for evermore. Amen' was not a man who understood fellowship.

Verse 45 shows us this fellowship in action. Selling their possessions and goods, they gave to anyone as he had need. This leads some to suppose they were a commune. Does it mean that every Spirit-filled Christian has to realize his capital and give it all away? We should not rule that out. Some people may be called to do just that. The rich young ruler was in Matthew 19:16–22 and there have been others in every generation since. But if you look at verse 46, you will find that they did not *all* sell their homes. Instead, we find them breaking bread in their homes, eating together with glad and sincere hearts.

Then in Acts 5, when the judgement of God fell on Ananias and Sapphira, you find there that Peter says that it was entirely at their discretion whether or not they sold their property and how much they gave away.

> Ananias, how is it that Satan has so filled your heart that you have lied to the Holy Spirit and have kept for yourself some of the money you received for the land? Didn't it belong to you before it was sold? And after it was sold, wasn't the money at your disposal? What made you think of doing such a thing? You have not lied to men but to God (Acts 5:3, 4).

It was Ananias' land and his money. The judgement that came on him, such that he fell down and died, was not on his greed but on his hypocrisy, because he lied to the Holy Spirit. There was no levy on the early Christians to give away everything they had. Nor was there any compulsion on them to do that for, as Paul says, God loves a cheerful (literally a hilarious) giver (2 Cor 9:7).

So let us be careful when we talk about the practicalities of fellowship. To see ownership as the root of all evil is a Marxist doctrine, not a Christian position. What is distinctively Christian is to share all that we have, generously, with others. So back in Acts 2:45, they sold their possessions and gave to anyone as he had need. That is Christian. The same thing occurs in Acts 4:34–35: 'There were no needy persons among them. For from time to time those who owned land or houses sold them, brought the money from the sales and put it at the apostles' feet, and it was distributed to anyone as he had need.' We can see how they cared for people in Acts 6:1. 'In those days when the number of disciples was increasing, the Grecian Jews among them complained against those of the Aramaic-speaking community because their widows were being overlooked in the daily distribution of food.'

Their fellowship expressed itself in personal care that was detailed and daily. There is a real danger that because we live in a Welfare State we, as Christians, ignore our continuing responsibilities in this matter. But there are still plenty of people in all sorts of need. Christians must be most enthusiastic about sharing. Whether it is property, so that our homes are open homes, or possessions so that all we have is at Christ's disposal for him to use. If I have a car and can use it to pick somebody up to bring them to church, part of my fellowship is that I do it. Whether it is our money or our time, our energy or our talents or our love, giving it away to other people is the Christian way of doing it. Jesus says you will receive a thousandfold. So every church ought to be committed to this priority, to our being a society of generous givers, not greedy grabbers. Sharing is our motto.

The nationalized energy industries have made famous their motto, 'Save it'. The church should have everywhere as her motto: 'Share it'. I am so glad that Christians in our churches are learning at last that this does not simply entail refreshments after the service or a handshake at the door. We belong to one another. We do not own one another. We all have private lives and personal choices, and that is absolutely right and proper, but we need more of the love that goes out of its way to care for one another; a fellowship that always thinks the best of my brother, that refuses to be suspicious, or envious, or spiteful.

Thirdly, they were committed to worship. This is expanded for us in Acts 2:46: 'Every day they continued to meet together in the temple courts. They broke bread in their homes and ate together with glad and sincere hearts,

praising God and enjoying the favour of all the people.'
Here is a blend of the formal and the informal. They kept
up their attendance at the temple. Peter and John were on
their way into the temple for the afternoon time of prayer,
when they encountered the cripple at the Beautiful Gate
(Acts 3:1, 2). They wanted to be part of the temple service. They also used the temple courts for their larger
gatherings. But Acts 2:46 tells us that they met in home
groups as well, which was inevitable as they were now
well over 3,000 in membership. Think of how many home
groups you would need for that number! And we need
home groups in our churches because without small units
of supportive fellowship, none of us will develop spiritually as fully as we might. If you are not a part of a small
group, where you can give and receive, you are depriving
yourself of one of God's major means of growth.

Furthermore the quality of their worship was glad and
sincere, both joyful and reverent. There was an awe in
their lives because God was in their midst. But there was a
great joy about it as well. We need both of those qualities
in our corporate worship.

Sometimes evangelical Christians seem to be afraid of
silence in worship. Other traditions within the church
know more about that than we do. We desperately need a
greater sense of awe among us because the Holy Spirit can
be as much in the silence as in the volume. But either way,
worship is to be a priority. Take 'breaking of bread'. We
need to have as one of our concerns being at the Lord's
table as often as we can. Again we need to meet regularly
with other Christians to pray, and to be committed to
that. It is a great privilege to be able to make time to pray
with other Christians at least once during the week, on a
regular basis. We do not need to be inhibited about this.
We love one another and we belong together. It is the
most natural expression of our fellowship to get together
and share our mutual concerns with the Lord.

And lastly, evangelism: 'And the Lord added to their number daily those who were being saved' (Acts 2:47b). To what sort of church did God add new Christians? One that had its priorities clear? That is correct. But look at verse 47a: 'Praising God and enjoying the favour of all the people.' God added to a church that was attractive to people. This church enjoyed the favour of those who were not yet Christians. It was a lively, magnetic group of people. Others liked what they saw. To hear some Christians speak today you would think that attractiveness was a mark of unfaithfulness. If the world looks at the church and likes what it sees, they imply that that church must be very unsound.

Let us bury for ever the myth that if a church's life is attractive it cannot be faithful. That was never true! This church was an attractive church to people who were not yet Christian. Pray that God will make your church like that. I recently heard of a man who had been in my church one summer. He wrote to thank people for providing such a welcome for him. He especially appreciated the personal care shown to him in a comparatively large congregation. It was a great encouragement to us, because that is what people ought to be finding. Never grow weary in well-doing.

The way in which the early church won people was through living Christlike lives. They overflowed Jesus to people and the Lord did the adding because, as we saw in the previous chapter, true evangelism is God-centred. Nor did the Lord just add converts. He added disciples and he did it daily. Just as their worship was daily, so their evangelism was daily. Just as they were praying and sharing together day by day, so they were overflowing the life of Jesus, day by day. It was a way of life that was continuous, and to that church the Lord added those who were being saved.

I fear that many of us Christians are still appallingly self-centred. We spend an enormous amount of time looking in on our problems. We can become very introspective personally and ingrown as communities. But God wants us to turn around to see the world of need in which he has placed us. A happy church is one that is giving and going, one that is reaching out, that does not have time to think how it feels today, because it is in the business of sharing the life of Jesus with the world in which Christ has placed it. And that should be the purpose of our fellowship. We do not just gather together as the be all and end all of everything. We gather to scatter. You do not go to church on Sunday morning only in order to have a good time together with other Christians. You go in order to penetrate your world during the week, more effectively for Christ. We are not to devote all our resources to pampering ourselves. The church is not a health farm, nor is it a beauty parlour. The church is a battle hospital. Check your priorities!

5

How Does a Church Mature?

In a consumer society like ours, we are used to selecting a model from a range of goods, according to our assessment of its quality, design, performance and price. Almost without realizing it, we can import the same selection procedure into our view of the church. We buy in to the model which attracts us most. That process is not necessarily wrong. It may actually be unavoidable, but it should not be unconscious. We need to be aware of what our own model of the church is and why we hold to it. Clearly this is important, because it will condition our involvement in the church, whether the church worldwide or its local expression, and also our relationship to other Christians within the body of Christ.

For some people, their model of the church is a one-man band—the expert. He used to be a common sight on street corners with a harmonica that he played with his mouth, drums that he managed somehow with his feet and cymbals strapped between his knees, which he banged together, and an accordion perhaps that he played with his fingers.

A similar model of the church which many people have is that of the circus juggler who spins plates at the ends of sticks. In order to keep them spinning, he runs along the line, giving them each a twirl, and then dashes back to the beginning and spins them again. Once more, it is a one-man show. Many seem to think of the church like that. They divide it between the performers and the spectators, and so when they turn up to the public performance, called the service, they come either to marvel at how the professionals do it, or to criticize their failures. It is a model that has no involvement and no responsibility. The church is defined purely in terms of what goes on in its public worship services on Sunday. This view reaches its peak in the United States where drive-in movies and drive-through take-aways have led to drive-in churches. Indeed you can drive into a car lot and see a church service transmitted on a huge television screen. I was told that over the entrance to one of these places is the inviting slogan: 'Worship God in the privacy of your own automobile.'

Ephesians 4 shatters that sort of thinking, thinking which belongs more to our western individualism than to biblical Christianity. So that model is out. The church is not a one-man band.

Some people see the church in terms of a supporters' club. They moved beyond the spectators to being the supporters. You can always rely on them being there on the touchline, every Sunday. They appreciate the finer points of the game. They are very ready to shout advice and to tell those who are playing on the field how to do it. But offer them some kit, ask them to join the training sessions and get stuck in with the team, and they will find a hundred-and-one reasons why they cannot. Are you a supporters' club Christian? A team will never win its matches if we are all non-playing captains. Ephesians 4 shatters that image of the church too, because it says to us we are in it together, and if we are not actively involved, then we have no evidence that we really belong to the body of Christ at all.

Next there is the conservationist model, which sees the modern church as an extension of the New Testament, but envisages its main purpose as to preserve the past for the present and future generations. The aim is to keep as much as unchanged as possible so we can see it all as it used to be, when people once lived in it. So it is beautifully preserved, but lifeless. This is a National Trust view of the church, in which it ends up by becoming a museum. If conservationism is your model of the church, Ephesians 4 shatters that image too, because it has an emphasis on change. The church is a living organism not a static organization. It must grow and develop, so change is built in. We are happy with this in terms of our physical life, so why not with our spiritual experience in the church?

So what is the church, and how does it mature? Paul answers these questions in Ephesians 4:11–16, one of the most important New Testament passages about the nature of the church:

> It was he [the ascended Christ] who gave some to be apostles, some to be prophets, some to be evangelists, and some to be pastors and teachers, to prepare God's people for works of service, so that the body of Christ may be built up until we all reach unity in the faith and in the knowledge of the Son of God and become mature, attaining to the whole measure of the fulness of Christ. Then we will no longer be infants, tossed back and forth by the waves, and blown here and there by every wind of teaching and by the cunning and craftiness of men in their deceitful scheming. Instead, speaking the truth in love, we will in all things grow up into him who is the Head, that is, Christ. From him the whole body, joined and held together by every supporting ligament, grows and builds itself up in love, as each part does its work.

In this passage Paul constantly challenges our individualism, by using plurals all the way through. Whatever he teaches about the mature church, he shows that you cannot reach that situation solo. The chapter challenges our complacency with its image of a body that is vibrant with life, one which, because it is always growing, is always changing. A mature church is a church that realizes how much more maturing has to be done. It has put aside the false concept of young Christians and mature Christians as though there is a point where you stop being a young Christian and you have now arrived and become a mature Christian. It is in fact a mark of immaturity to think like that. A mature church realizes that we are all in God's kindergarten together and that we all desperately need to be growing up into Christ.

We can examine what Paul teaches in Ephesians 4 in three ways. Firstly, there is the model of maturity—the right model that Paul puts before us under the inspiration of the Holy Spirit, for us to learn. Verse 13: 'Until we all reach unity in the faith and in the knowledge of the Son of God and become mature, attaining to the whole measure of the fulness of Christ.' Notice that the concept is both corporate and dynamic. *We* are growing. I cannot be a maturing Christian, unless I am contributing my part to the maturing of my fellow Christians in the body of Christ. But again, Paul's point is that the church is not a human organization, but a living organism. A body that does not grow is abnormal and so it is with the church. A human body expands in size, increases in strength, develops in ability, and the same thing is true of the church as the body of Christ. But there is a crucial difference. In human physical life, we are accustomed to reaching what we are pleased to call maturity, after which we know we are subject to decay, at least physically. There is a point at which age takes over. We are subject to all sorts of weaknesses that in the end lead to death.

But in the spiritual sphere, with the body of Christ, that is not so. There are no limits to its continuous growth. And so we are not to settle down to what we like to call maturity and imagine we can be content with where we are as Christians, or complacent about what our church is. There is always more growing and more building to be done. The mature church knows that it has not arrived, but that it is pressing on to the unity of the faith until we all come to the fulness of the knowledge of God, the whole measure of the stature of the fulness of Christ.

So I want to encourage you to do away with the idea that one day you will be a fully mature Christian. Unless by that you mean what Paul means at the end of verse 13, that one day you will obtain the whole measure of the fulness of Christ. He is our model for maturity and nothing less is acceptable to God.

Furthermore, verse 13 emphasizes that this development is a process. It speaks literally about our 'coming to meet' in unity of the faith and in our knowledge of God. The emphasis is on every Christian moving to a deeper unity with every other Christian, as we deepen our understanding of God's truth and our personal relationship with him. The emphasis is on *all* and on *unity*, so that we cannot escape the corporate nature of the model. If one member of the body is excluded from growth, then none of us is maturing as we should be. Therefore, all of us as Christians have responsibilities spiritually towards one another. Part of my Christian commitment is that I am to some extent responsible for my fellow Christians, for their growth and instruction, their health and encouragement. In turn, they are responsible for mine. No church can be maturing if it is not increasing in unity, for the aim is to be (literally) a 'complete man', attaining to the whole measure of the fulness of Christ.

Paul makes clear that you cannot be that sort of Christian or that sort of church unless together you are growing, unless each member is increasingly knowing and experiencing more of Christ and so building into the body by their contribution, through their presence, sharing with

others, their conversation, their encouragement, their
prayers, their giving and their serving. If we disagree
about what our priorities or our programme should be,
the church cannot mature or expand. But the model in
verse 13 provides an illustration for us of two ways in
which we can grow and in which we can become more
and more like Jesus, because as you read it carefully you
will see that Paul says that spiritual growth to maturity
comes by increasingly trusting and knowing Christ. It is
unity in the faith and in the knowledge of the Son of God.
If you take those two goals and turn them into verbs, you
are talking about trusting and knowing. The aim of the
church is its maturity in unity. That, says Paul, comes
from faith in Christ and from knowledge of him. Bringing
it down to practical terms for you and me today, we get to
know the Lord Jesus better as we receive and respond to
his word in the Bible and learn his requirements for our
lives. Then, as we respond to him in prayer and open up
each part of our lives to his grace and power, as we trust
him more by becoming obedient to him and by asking
him to rule in our decisions, we grow. We become
increasingly like Christ as individuals.

Also, we grow as a body, because as each individual is
growing, the whole body becomes stronger and more
united in the faith and knowledge of the Son of God. As
we grow, we are able to help and strengthen one another
and to reach out effectively to those who as yet do not
know the grace of God. It is a very simple picture, but
those two essentials of trust and knowledge are the means
by which the body is built. All the resources come from
the Head—from the one who is called in verse 13 Son of
God, the Christ. The more we each live in union with
Christ, the more together we cultivate and exemplify this
unity of thought, action and character, which is the sign of
an increasing maturity in the church.

If a church is full of people who are falling out with one

another and disagreeing or warring against each other, in terms of what the church ought to be doing or the way in which the church ought to be going, then it is obviously not a maturing church. The church at Corinth was like that. Paul had to say that they were 'mere infants' (1 Cor 3:1). The mark of maturity is a unity in truth, trusting Christ, knowing him and in building one another towards the whole measure of his fulness.

Secondly, Paul describes in verses 11 and 12 the means by which the maturity is to be achieved. It was the risen, ascended Christ, 'who gave some to be apostles, some to be prophets, some to be evangelists, and some to be pastors and teachers, to prepare God's people for works of service, so that the body of Christ may be built up'. Just as Christ is the source of life, so he is also the initiator of the process of growth. He is our goal, but he is also our source. One of the biblical meanings of the word 'head' is source, just as we might say the head of a river is the source of that river. Thus, verse 13 is not set before us as a wonderful but unattainable ideal. It is no mere theory. Verses 11 and 12 indicate how the church can increasingly achieve that aim. Paul takes us back to the ascension of Christ, the event which he sees as the necessary pre-requisite for the gifts of God's grace, through the Holy Spirit, to be given to men. It is the ascended Lord who provides for his church the resources it needs, in order to become the maturing community he designed it to be.

Christ's ascension demonstrated and proved his total victory over all the hostile powers that were ranged against us. Sin, death and the devil are all defeated in the cross, the resurrection and the ascension of the Lord Jesus. So whatever area of the universe we are thinking about, it is Jesus Christ who is Lord and Master there (verses 9 and 10). Jesus has stamped his authority on the earthly regions, by demonstrating his lordship in his perfect, blameless, human life. He has declared his victory to the imprisoned spirits in Hades, awaiting the ultimate judgement of God's wrath (1 Pet 3:19). He has ascended into the highest heavens and is now seated with the Father in majesty and limitless power, to fill the whole universe with his glory. Whether it is in the depths or in the heavens, Jesus is sovereign and he is the Lord who fills everything.

Moreover, this ascended Lord who has all authority and power gives gifts of grace to all his children: 'to each one of us grace has been given as Christ apportioned it' (Eph 4:7). Then, in verse 11, Paul explains how that works out in a church context. To enable his church to mature, Christ gave apostles, prophets, evangelists, pastors and teachers. Notice it is the past tense Paul uses. This implies a once-for-all decision to supply all the church needs, in every age, for God's will to be done and his plans to be fulfilled.

Personally, I believe that the gifts of the apostles and prophets were foundation gifts for the church. In Ephesians 2:20, Paul has spoken of the church as God's household, 'built on the foundation of the apostles and prophets, with Christ Jesus himself as the chief corner-stone'. The primary reference there is to those who were uniquely commissioned by the risen Lord. An apostle was somebody who had seen the risen Jesus (1 Cor 9:1) and who was sent out by him with a very specific mission to fulfil. A prophet was a channel of divine revelation before the New Testament was written and the canon of Scripture was complete. Together, the apostles and prophets constituted the foundation ministries, the authority upon which the church was built, with Jesus Christ as the chief cornerstone. The question is frequently put, 'Are those ministries not applicable and available today?' I would want to say that these ministries are indeed available to us, but in Scripture. For the apostles and prophets who were the channels of revelation, under the influence of the Spirit, committed to writing what we call the New Testament—the apostolic faith and practice. In Scripture we have the clear unchanging revelation of the mind and will of God, the explicit foundation on which the church is built; God's truth for all time. Whatever claims may be made about the role of apostles and prophets today, ultimately, all their utterances must be tested at the bar of the Scriptures. They are not self-constituted authorities, or channels of fresh revelations. They must be equally under the authority of Scripture if they are to be true to Christ, for what God has once said, he is still saying. In that sense, the ministry of these foundation gifts ceased with the completion of the New Testament and it only confuses the issue to apply these titles to gifts of missionary evangelism, church planting, teaching or exhortation today.

But while there may be controversy about the role of the prophets today, there is little controversy about evangelists, pastors and teachers. The evangelists stand between the foundation of the universal church and the formation of new local Christian churches. The evangelist is the one who brings the truth of the apostolic gospel, proclaiming it in the power of the Holy Spirit, so that men and women respond to that message and become Christians, by repentance towards God and faith in the Lord Jesus Christ. As new Christians are built into the body of Christ, that community will need a shepherd, which is what the word 'pastor' means. So the pastor-teacher (the two terms belong together) is provided to look after and nurture the flock, by feeding them on the pure word of God's truth.

All of these are Christ's gifts to the church. They are not produced by the church. They are not employees of the church. They are given to it by the Head of the church, who is the Lord. But here too, the concept of ministry within the body is never static. In other words, the New Testament is never concerned with appointing people to office, but with their spiritual function. The work of these gifted leaders in the church, says Paul, is never an end in itself. The aim of the pastor-teacher is not just to care for and feed the sheep. There is a greater goal to which he is working. Verse 12 says his role is to prepare God's people for works of service, so that the body of Christ may be built up. There is a throughput that Paul is concerned about. He is interested in the whole people of God, so he writes that these gifts have particular functions in the church and are given primarily so that the whole body may be prepared for its work of service (*diakonia*). This has given us our English word 'deacon', which we have come to associate with a particular office in the church. But Paul's point is that the whole church is made up of deacons. Everyone in it is to be committed to the work of ministering. Indeed, that ministry of every member of the body is essential if the body is to grow.

So when the old hymn says, 'There's a work for Jesus, none but you can do,' it is absolutely true. Your role is absolutely vital to the church. God wants to prepare every one of his people for works of service, so that the body of Christ may be built up. And if we are not active in his service, we are not contributing to the growth of that body. It is significant to note that the verb that is used here 'to prepare' God's people is the same verb used in the gospels about mending nets. It means to put something together in such a way that it can be used, to bring things to a state of readiness. That, states Paul, is his ministry as an apostle. It is the ministry of the evangelist, as well as that of the pastor and the teacher, to bring the people of God into a state of readiness so that they are able to do their personal work of ministry, to which every Christian is called and must be committed. The task of what we call the ordained minister, or a full-time elder, is primarily to be in the supplies division. If you do not have a supplies division, your army cannot advance. Nothing ever gets through to it. On the front they will be starved if there are no supplies coming from behind. Similarly the role of the full-time ministry, if we call it that, is to supply, through the teaching and pastoring, what is needed by every Christian for their work of service.

Next, the role of the Christian out there in the secular world, on the frontline for Christ, is building up the body of Christ. How can that happen? There are many ingredients. As Christians, we want to have a distinctive input to our everyday work, in terms of doing our job to the very best of our ability. But beyond that, we shall want to share our faith with colleagues, neighbours, acquaintances as natural contacts and opportunites develop through our ordinary life in the world. But we are not lone rangers! We need to be strengthened, by regularly being fed from God's word, to be encouraged by the fellowship of others who are also in the learning process of discipleship, and to be stimulated to live for Christ in our bit of his world, realizing that an impact can be made for him through our lives.

If you appreciate being taught God's truth, if you appreciate pastoral care, if too you appreciate fellowship in the body of Christ, let me ask you, why do you want it? The only valid reason biblically is so that you may serve. That is the point. When you start to exercise, your body grows stronger. If you fail to, you just grow lazy. It is also true spiritually and our service has a very distinct aim according to Ephesians 4:12. It is so that the body of Christ may be built. In other words, no church can grow, unless *all* its members are using their God-given gifts of service, which the Lord of the church has dispensed to each of us in some way, because we are all recipients of his grace (verse 7). Every one of us has a spiritual gift, so that we can all make a contribution. He has given it to us all, so that we may build up others.

Moreover, the importance or validity of those gifts does

not depend on any particular function or role or office in the church, other than whether or not they build up the body of Christ. The word of God is the agent that gives growth through the power of the Holy Spirit. Our gifts need to be exercised under the authority of that word and that spirit, to strengthen, encourage and build up others. Every member is in the ministry.

Therefore, the old division between the clergy and the laity is a totally unbiblical one. We *all* have something to contribute. You set aside certain people within a church in order to be a supplies division, so that the church may be fed or pastored and that it may be strong for the work of the ministry in the world. We sometimes talk about the priesthood of all believers. I want to encourage all of you reading this to believe equally in the ministry of all believers. If you are not yet a serving Christian, then it is of the utmost importance that you discover your gifts and start to use them in the church. Go to one of the spiritual leaders in your own church to talk this through. Ask them to help you realistically to assess how God has equipped you to serve the body and then find the niche he has for you and start working, as soon as you can.

Lastly, verses 14–16 describe the marks of maturity. These are very important verses. How do we know we are maturing as Christians? Is it if we feel good? If I feel okay is that all right? That is not what the Bible teaches. Am I maturing as a Christian if I can recite so many bible verses? Well, that can be a help but it is not a mark of spiritual maturity, simply one of a good memory. Nor can I measure maturity according to my doctrinal knowledge, or the quantity and scope of my Christian activities. These verses give a picture of the maturity that we should long to see as increasingly characteristic of the church. We need to get the right marks. Verse 14: 'Then we will no longer be infants, tossed back and forth by the waves, and blown here and there by every wind of teaching and by the cunning and craftiness of men in their deceitful scheming.'

The alternative to being mature says Paul is a continuing childishness, which is nothing short of tragic. We are to be like children in our total dependence on God our heavenly Father, but here Paul focuses on aspects of childish behaviour, which really ought not to characterize those who are called grown-ups. The two things he focuses on are ignorance and instability.

He says that the marks of children are that they are very easily distracted and diverted. Those of you who know children need no convincing about that! They find concentration very difficult because concentration has to be learned by practice. It is the mark of children that they want to be entertained by the latest fashion, and that often continues well into adolescence. But Peter Pan is not a Christian ideal. Refusal to grow up is not the Christian way of looking at things. Sadly though, some Christians are like spiritual children or adolescents even after years of Christian experience. They are like a boat on a stormy sea, blown around by all the newest fads and fancies of the Christian fringe culture; tossed back and forth by the waves, blown here and there by every wind of teaching. They are people who are easily deceived, Paul writes, by crafty men who exploit them to create a following for themselves. Such men are cunning, deceitful schemers. The picture in the original is of a cheat, playing with loaded die. To fall for that, Paul makes clear, is not a mark of maturity. There are Christians who are prepared to sing any old rubbish if the tune is attractive. They are prepared to believe any old teaching, or any new teaching, if it is presented powerfully enough. They are prepared to respond to all sorts of emotional pressures because they have no stability. But, says Paul, do not be content to stay like that. God means something much better for you.

Verse 15: 'Instead, speaking the truth in love.' Our translation is very unfortunate here because there is no

verb in the original about speaking, so it is rather mislead-
ing. The better, more literal translation which gets across
what Paul means is 'truthing it in love', because truth is the
verb in the original. So, he says, instead of this instability
and ignorance, 'I want you to be Christians who truth it in
love.' Those are the two marks of maturity which he says
are indispensable—truth and love. The church cannot be a
maturing church without truth. You cannot grow as a
Christian without teaching. But neither can it be mature
without love, for verse 16 tells us that it is in love that the
church grows and builds itself up. So these are not
alternatives—truth or love—both have to be cultivated
together. They are marks of maturity which each should
long to see as personal and then corporate characteristics.

By nature, we tend to polarize one way or the other.
Some of us are more emotional people: others more
cerebral, and our personality tends to move us in one of
the two directions. We tend to say, 'I am a truth Christian,' or 'I am a love Christian.' There are some who say it
is the mind that matters and others that it is the heart that
counts. There are some who major on doctrine and others
who emphasize experience. There are some who always
emphasize the word and others who always emphasize the
Spirit.

But if you polarize these two essentials, you cannot
claim to be mature. It is maturity to recognize that
growing up into Christ means truthing it in love. It means
having both those ingredients integrated within us. It is no
use having all the right doctrine if you do not have a
vibrant experience of Christ. But it is equally no use
having a heart that is just full of love, for it would be
merely sentiment, if your mind is not being taught by
truth. Truth becomes hard if it is not softened by love and
love becomes soft if it is not strengthened by truth. So,
maturing Christians, says Paul, are those who are becoming more like Jesus by resolutely holding these two

ingredients together.

There is no other way to mature unity. Just as the body of Christ cannot exist without the truth, nor can it exist unless those who believe in the truth love one another. That is what we Christians ought to dedicate ourselves to, as we are growing up into Christ: 'From him the whole body, joined and held together by every supporting ligament, grows and builds itself up in love, as each part does its work' (Eph 4:16). When that is happening God will make the body grow in numbers, and God will build the body up in strength. Our responsibility is to make sure that each part is doing its work. As we work together, love grows and we build one another up into Christ.

If you are a committed Christian, are you doing your part? Have you realized that you are in living contact with the Head and you are part of the supporting ligaments? You have got something to contribute. Your prayers, your love, your care, your service—they all matter if the whole body is to be growing and building itself up in love. But it is only when *each* part is working properly that this can happen. If you feel a particularly tired ligament, or especially weary at the moment, remember that Christ is the source of all spiritual life and energy. He is the Head, the one who has all the necessary supplies for every member and every limb.

And if, through you, the life of Christ is flowing, you will find that he will revive, refresh and renew you, so as to enable you to make that contribution. When your human physical strength is at an end, he will give you more grace, more ability, more of his gifts, for through the whole body the pulse of God's love is to be experienced. And love goes on giving and giving. As Bishop Handley Moule expressed it:

To know and do the Head's commands
For this the body lives and grows.
All speed of feet and skill of hands
Is for Him spent and from Him flows.

6

In Good Working Order

Therefore, I urge you, brothers, in view of God's mercy, to offer your bodies as living sacrifices, holy and pleasing to God—which is your spiritual worship. Do not conform any longer to the pattern of this world, but be transformed by the renewing of your mind. Then you will be able to test and approve what God's will is—his good, pleasing and perfect will. For by the grace given me I say to every one of you: Do not think of yourself more highly than you ought, but rather think of yourself with sober judgment, in accordance with the measure of faith God has given you. Just as each of us has one body with many members, and these members do not all have the same function, so in Christ we who are many form one body, and each member belongs to all the others. We have different gifts, according to the grace given us. If a man's gift is prophesying, let him use it in proportion to his faith. If it is serving, let him serve; if it is teaching, let him teach; if it is encouraging, let him encourage; if it is contributing to the needs of others, let him give generously; if it is leadership, let him govern diligently; if it is showing mercy, let him do it cheerfully (Rom 12:1-8).

One of the most instructive contrasts of the New Testament is that which sets the church over against the world. The New Testament talks about those who are in Christ and those who are in Adam. All of us are born in Adam, sharing from the beginning his form and human nature. This means that no human being is born morally perfect. The story of human life is not one of unfortunate failure but of a human will which is bent in going in the wrong moral direction and determined not to do God's will. We inherit what we call 'original sin', which simply means that everyone who is born into the world is a sinner, by nature.

There are, however, those who are in Christ, those who because of the work of the Lord Jesus on the cross and in their lives have been saved, or redeemed from sin. They have now become Christians and as the New Testament makes clear their lifestyle, basic outlook and purpose are in strong contrast to those who are still in Adam.

This is one of the great themes in the letter to the Romans. Paul describes it there as the contrast between the old order and the new. He says that the Christian is someone who has been given life by the Spirit of Christ within him, and that the Holy Spirit produces a radically different lifestyle. The church, the living body of Christians meeting together, is to be the locus where both can be observed and experienced.

We are accustomed, in our western individualism, to think of verses 1 and 2 of Romans 12 as a great appeal for personal holiness. Almost all of us instinctively read 'you' in the singular. But, of course, in the original, all these pronouns are plural. But while there is an appeal for individual holiness here, because the holiness of the church depends upon the holiness of the Christian, the dominant perspective of Paul's writing is plural. He is thinking about the church as a unity or an entity. We have to offer our bodies, verse 1 says. We do that individually to God. Our minds need to be renewed, says verse 2, by God's truth every day, and that is a personal action. But it has corporate effects. This is God's plan for his church, his pattern for us all, because verse 2 states that the danger is that the church can look all too much like the world and be conformed to its patterns. J. B. Phillips paraphrases it this way: 'Don't let the world around you squeeze you into its own mould.' In other words, each of us lives in a world where there are pressures on us, and our corporate mind as the church, needs to be constantly renewed by God's truth, otherwise we shall merely reflect the spirit of the age. The best way to understand that expression for our own time is to see it largely in terms of a confidence in man, in our technology and methodology, in our ability to lick all our problems, if only we are given enough time and enough cash. But God said centuries ago, through the prophet Zechariah, that his work is achieved 'Not by might nor by power, but by my Spirit' (Zech 4:6).

The church is also often tempted to use what Paul calls in his Corinthian letter 'worldly weapons' (2 Cor 10:4), which means that we adopt this world's view of what is important and this world's style and methods to accomplish it. The church begins to think in terms of prestige, in terms of personalities and popularity. But as soon as we start to rely on anything fundamentally human, we cease to be the sort of church Jesus Christ wants. All that the church needs is in her Head, and therefore we are not to be conformed to the way the world thinks about values and purposes, but we are to be radically different because our minds are being renewed.

Verse 3 introduces the subject of all the members of the body working harmoniously. Here, Paul underlines a particular way in which we are tempted to be squeezed into the world's mould, in regard to the use of the gifts that God has given to every Christian. So he exhorts us in verse 3 not to think of ourselves more highly than we ought, but to have a sober judgement. In effect, he says, 'If you Christians are really going to fulfil God's pattern of body life, you have got to think differently. Your minds have to be transformed.'

There are two ways in which the church can experience this pressure from the world. The first is by becoming downright apathetic and lazy. There are Christians who really could not care less about the contribution they are making to the body of Christ. And of course, those who never stop and think about it are unlikely to be contributing very much to God's church. Some while ago now, there was an interesting survey mentioned on the radio which had been carried out among a cross-section of British workers. Various people in different industries and professions had been asked, 'Do you want to do a thoroughly good job day by day?' The staggering result was that the number of people who replied positively to that question was only 17%.

You can get that sort of worldly thinking in the church. It often masquerades there as a form of humility. It says, 'Oh, I don't have any gifts; don't ask me to do it.' There may be a job to be done but we are really not interested in carrying out that sort of thing. What that usually means is that we cannot be bothered to take on the responsibility or we are not prepared to be committed to something on a regular basis. We just do not want to be accountable. We like our freedom to do what we like when we feel like it. That is exactly what I mean about the spirit of the age infecting the church. But the authentic Christian response, as given in verse 6, is just the opposite: 'We have different gifts, according to the grace given us.' And every Christian is gifted by God to fulfil the role that he or she has been allotted in the church. So do not let the world squeeze you into its way of apathy. Whether you do the job or not, it *does* matter to God and it matters to his body.

The other extreme into which the world would like to squeeze us is that of trying to do everything. This is the opposite error, not of lazy inactivity, but of carnal pride; one which says, 'If I don't do it, it won't be done properly.' This can easily happen in a church. If you have responsibilities, you will be tempted to take on more of them yourself, because in the world the rule is you use your talents to win power or promotion or status, or whatever it may be, and to build up number one. But in the church, you are not building up yourself, but are using the talents and gifts which God has given you to build up others. It is a fundamentally different concept. Do not use your gifts, says Paul, to minister to yourself.

There is a very easy way in which we can tell whether we are guilty of that or not. If we are using our gifts in the wrong way, we continually smart when we are not recognized by people for what we are doing. When you have done something 'for the Lord' and it has not been recognized by anybody, if there is something inside you that hurts and says, 'I would have thought someone might have had the decency to say thank you,' then that is a pretty good sign that you are using your gifts to minister to yourself rather than to the Lord, to inflate yourself rather than equip his body.

We need to be realistic and ruthlessly honest about this, because all of us can use our gifts to build up our own self-image and end up by serving our own ends rather than the Lord or his people. The sober judgement that verse 3 talks about means choosing not to strive to be everything, because we recognize that only Christ can be that; nor sitting back and letting everybody else do it, because we recognize that there is a unique task that each of us has to accomplish for him. On the last night of his earthly life, Jesus was able to say to his Father in heaven, 'I have finished the work you gave me to do' (Jn 17:4); no more, no less. It is a testimony of commitment and balance that we would all do well to covet. Sober judgement, however, means saying 'I am just a member of this body, and however gifted I may be, however great or small my task may be, I am and always will be supremely a member of the body.' It is not your church; it is not my church; it is Christ's church. I am not the head; you are not the head; he is the Head.

So as we look at using our gifts, we have come to realize that it is all too easy for spiritual gifts to be exercised in a worldly and unspiritual way. That was the trouble at Corinth. But spiritual gifts are not given for us to minister to ourselves. They are to build up the whole body of Christ and that is how the unity of the church, which is at the heart of God's pattern, begins to work. Paul tells us that we have daily to offer our bodies to God as living sacrifices (verse 1). If I want my gifts to be used in a spiritual way, that will begin every day that I say to the Lord, 'Lord, you have given me this day to live in. It is a gift from you. I have life and breath and your measure of health and strength. I want to live this day, in the world, for your glory. And so I offer myself to you, Lord Jesus, as a living sacrifice—not to die but to live for you.'

But the use of that word 'sacrifice' is significant, because there are two important aspects to it. A sacrifice has no will of its own and it has no future plans of its own. Therefore, if I am going to offer my body as a living sacrifice, it means that as I start each day as a Christian, I dedicate all that I am to God. We may sometimes find it helpful consciously to give the constituent parts of our being to God, in prayer: 'Lord . . . here I am . . . your eyes to look through, your ears to listen to the aching world, your lips with which to speak, your mind to think, your hands to work, your feet to go wherever you want me. Today, Lord, may your will be done in me, your bit of earth, as it is in Jesus, who is my heaven.' Have you definitely ever given yourself to Jesus like that? If it is true of our daily lives as Christians then we are offering ourselves to God in a way which is holy and pleasing to him.

Paul then reminds us that there has to be a continuous

renewal of the mind (verse 2), so that we can war against those of the world's pressures which will try to make us conform. The mind is the most crucial area of our discipleship, the means through which we are to be daily renewed by God is his truth. Christians must have minds that are instructed by God's truth, not anaesthetized by television, or trivialized by secular culture. We are to give all of our minds to the whole of God's truth. Paul says that if you dedicate your bodies to God and actively allow your minds to be renewed day by day, through reading and studying the Scriptures, you will come to understand that God's will is good and pleasing and perfect. You will also be the sort of Christian in the body of Christ who can contribute, because you are in touch with the Lord, the Head. You will be at his disposal, thinking his thoughts with your mind, and your life will be moving in his direction.

Then thirdly, you will come (verse 3) to a right estimate of yourself. This will enable you to realize that all we have is a gift from God and that it is our great privilege to be faithful stewards of everything God has first given to us. When you come to a right estimate of yourself, you realize that any gift you have is not due to your merit, but to God's grace. All the gifts flow from a God who is gracious and merciful and loving. Paul teaches that it is only as we live both personally and then corporately in this pattern of active involvement in the church that the body of Christ can really function as the Maker designed it. That places a solemn responsibility on each of us and on us all together; that we really mean business with God in our discipleship.

Next, in verses 4–8, Paul goes on to describe God's provision for each of us. The unity of the church is created partly by the similarity of the members—we are all of equal value to the Head—but it is also very important to realize that we all have a specific task to fulfil. So within the fundamental unity there is a great diversity, as verses 4 and 5 show us: 'Just as each of us has one body with many members, and these members do not all have the same function, so in Christ we who are many form one body, and each member belongs to all the others.' Now, that could lead to the destruction of the body by disintegration, unless each of the members follows God's pattern. Paul is teaching that each Christian has his own gifts to contribute to the well-being of the whole, and therefore of himself.

If you injure the body, or if you as an individual Christian fail to pull your weight in the body, you injure and frustrate yourself. For God has designed you within the body, in order that you might find your fulfilment there. As a pastor, people sometimes come to me and say, 'I really feel as though I am not part of the church. My Christian life isn't what it used to be; it's going downhill and I don't know why.' The reason can be quite easy to find. Sometimes, but not always, it is because they are not contributing anything. If you are not fulfilling your role in the body, you will feel frustrated and that your Christian life is not achieving anything. Paul is not just using a poetic metaphor. He is affirming that the body of Christ is an indisputable reality. If we belong to Christ we are fitted into that body, and we are to demonstrate our unity by each part working properly, within our diversity. So, he says in verse 6, we have different gifts. The word there is 'grace' gifts or *charismata*. In that sense, we are all charismatic Christians, because *every* Christian has a gift of God's grace. God has equipped us to fulfil a particular function. Our love for one another is seen in our faithful stewardship of the gifts he has given. So whatever your gift is, he has not given it primarily for your personal enjoyment any more than the gift is one of your personal choice. It is *God* who decides what gift you have and he has given you that gift (or whatever gifts you may have, as many have more than one) in order that you may fulfil the role that he has designed for you within his church. That is the reason why it is so foolish and destructive to envy somebody else's gift. So many people sit down, wasting time, wishing they were others. Paul is telling us to get on with using the gift we have and as we use that gift and do our part in the body, so we shall find the fulfilment God designs specifically for us. No one is superfluous. Everyone counts. In that sense, everybody is indispensable because we are all needed in the body of Christ.

In verses 6–8 we find seven distinct gifts that are mentioned. We all know there are other lists in the New Testament, notably in 1 Corinthians 12 and Ephesians 4, which include other gifts. All together, the gifts specifically mentioned number around seventeen or eighteen, but there is no evidence in the New Testament that that is the limit. Here Paul selects different types of gifts that you might expect to find in any church. For example, he says in verse 6: 'If a man's gift is prophesying, let him use it in proportion to his faith.' The essence of prophesying is communicating God's revelation of truth. The prophet was God's spokesman. Before the New Testament was completed, the office of prophet in the church was one by which the revelation of God came, hence the prophet is to speak in proportion to his faith. My understanding of what Paul means here is that the prophet is not to go beyond what God gives him to speak. He is not to speak on his own authority, or out of his own desire, but, simply believing that God has directed him to speak, he is to speak the word up to the point to which God has given it and not beyond.

Similarly he is not to withhold the truth that God instructs him to proclaim. So prophecy means speaking God's word with God's authority and conviction into a contemporary situation. That is why I believe that all biblical preaching is rightly prophetic. But it must be judged by the written word of God, by Scripture which God has already spoken, because God will never speak a word today in conflict with his written revelation. We need to remember that. The idea that the prophet is a vehicle of fresh revelation is a very dangerous one. Some of us can think of examples where groups have begun which initially appeared to be orthodox and Christian, but where someone within the group acquired such a dominance over the others that that person became a 'prophet' in the sense that they claimed God was revealing new things to and through them. Then those who followed them very quickly became unorthodox and drifted into becoming a sect. Once an unorthodox belief is accepted, the way is open for all sorts of immoral behaviour to follow.

The church needs prophetic ministry, but through the written Scriptures, the word of God. I believe Paul places this gift so frequently at the top of his lists both because of its primary importance and its consequent responsibility. In the last chapter we saw that it was a foundation gift, alongside the apostles. To be a prophet in the New Testament church meant you were laying the foundation of truth. We now have that foundation in the New Testament itself, which forms the plumb-line by which all teaching and exhortation must be judged in the church today. Certainly we need prophetic ministry, but we also have to recognize that in its content it will be God's unchanging word of Scripture, spoken with truthful relevance and convicting power into our current situation, so that it moulds and shapes our believing and behaving. It is *the* great antidote to the world's suffocating bear-hug!

Then in verse 7 Paul describes a very important general gift which he calls 'serving'. The Greek verb gives us our word 'deacon', a term used in the New Testament both of ministering in the word and in practical helpfulness. But more usually it refers to all the practical gifts that are needed for any church fellowship to function and grow. This means it is not just the work of people who are designated as deacons, but more generally the work of all gifted Christians who are equipped by the Lord to be servers. You do not have to be elected to a committee in order to exercise the gift of deaconing, especially since the New Testament is always much more concerned with the function than with the office. It is not the status or label that counts but getting the job done. So Paul says here, if your gift is serving, serve! The church should recognize its gifted servants and allow them to devote their time to those particular areas for which they are equipped by God. Each time Paul says let people use their gift of prophecy saying . . . let them serve . . . let them teach . . . let them encourage, he is in effect telling the whole church to allow these people who have the gifts to exercise them in their midst. Ministry has to be received, as well as offered. But it is also exhorting the person who has the gift to make sure that they actually do what God has called them to do. With the gift of service, of course, it is not usually an open or particularly prominent gift and some people do not bother to exercise it. Or else they strive after doing other things, for which they are not gifted, but which may be more in the public eye. To such people Paul says in effect, 'Never mind whether it is in the public eye or not. That is utterly irrelevant. Faithfulness is all that matters and if your gift is quiet service, exercise that gift faithfully, wherever God has called you to do it.'

The next two gifts in verses 7 and 8 go together. They are teaching and encouraging, and one can see why they are related in practice. Teaching is a gift of making the truth of God clear and plain, one that is directed to the understanding. Encouragement directs that same word to the heart, to the conscience and to the will. Both are vitally necessary for the church to function, since it is both truth and love that are needed. So the teacher's task is not just to fill the mind with truth, but to apply it to the life, while the encourager's ministry is not just to stir the emotions, but to take the truth and use it to strengthen.

The last three gifts follow a different construction, and here Paul's concern is not so much with the gifts actually being used, as with the way in which they are exercised. It is equally important that they are put into effect in a spiritual way if these gifts are to build up the body. He talks about 'contributing to the needs of others' and he says in verse 8, 'let him give generously' (literally, with simplicity). It means with the unmixed motives that are characteristic of generous giving. If the reason is right, then the generosity will follow. We ought to ask ourselves whether we greet the arrival of the collection bag on Sunday with enthusiasm, because we are so overjoyed at the opportunity of giving generously to the Lord. That is the sort of cheerful giving God loves! But it is not simply thinking about the collection bag on Sunday, but of ways you can give to others; perhaps financially, maybe in other ways, such as using your home or other resources. Do it with an unmixed heart. Do it gladly. Do it generously. Paul says this because the danger of giving is that we do it with the ulterior motive of securing influence or personal advantage. But giving in a godly way is a wonderful ministry that God calls us all to exercise. You do not have to be rich to give generously. He is not thinking about quantity, but about the quality of our giving. In any case, the resources that any Christian has are all God's gifts. So we are only giving back to him what he loans to us, in order that it may be used for his glory. I think that sometimes God gives especially to those whom he can trust to give to others.

Next, Paul teaches that if you are gifted with leadership, you must govern 'diligently'. This shows there must be an oversight in the church, some control. The church must be governed diligently. Just as a shepherd has constantly to watch over his flock to protect it and provide pasture, so those who lead the church must constantly be vigilant. One danger is that church leaders can regard their gift as a sort of hobby, a purely part-time interest. For the gift to be exercised properly, energy and hard work, coupled with devotion, are required. That is why you need to pray for the elders or deacons or council in your church, or for the leader(s) of your Bible study group(s) that meet in homes, because they have leadership responsibilities and their task is to do it diligently. It is possible to over-react to the opposite extreme and to substitute for no leadership a heavy-handed domineering control over the lives of God's people, which is equally unbiblical (1 Pet 5:3). But the biblical perpendicular is for strong, loving, responsible leadership to be exercised in the church, to guard it from error and division, and to facilitate its growth. There also has to be a structure of government. The church is not a democracy, but a theocracy. Christ is its Head and while we are all of equal value in God's sight, some are given special responsibilites of leadership, for which they will have to give special account to God of their stewardship. Church discipline is a necessary feature of body life, as it is in any family or community, so that those who govern must not shirk their responsibilities.

Or, if your gift is showing mercy, 'let him do it cheerfully'. The thought here is of a more direct personal ministry to someone in need, and cheerfulness is all-important if it is to be a means of grace. Many of us have been visited by people who have come 'to do us good', as a duty, grudgingly, and usually wished that they had not bothered! Their hearts are not involved in it at all. Paul says to such people not to think that that is a spiritual gift; for it is nothing of the kind. Someone who has the gift of being merciful and loving is a person who will exercise that gift with joy. After all what validity does a ministry of mercy have if it is not done from a joyful heart?

So there are some of the representative gifts of God's grace which faith must develop by exercise. It is not a total list, because there are many others, but these are a good cross-section. They represent the major categories by which the body of Christ is to be built up. Some of them are word gifts—prophecy, teaching, encouraging. Some of them are very practical—serving, giving, showing mercy. But whatever they are, they are to be cultivated and exercised in order to build up the body in love. If you are committed to a church family (and every Christian should be) it means that you need to pray about what you are contributing to your church and to ask the Lord what it is he wants you to be doing. If you are in the right place, doing all that he wants you to do, you will come to that conviction about it. But for many of us, he may be calling us to do a little bit extra. He may be asking us to get more involved, to start to exercise gifts that have lain fallow or remained underdeveloped for too long. When we start to do that, then the body starts to grow and mature because every part is working properly.

To conclude this chapter, we need to examine what a church that is working properly looks like. This is to be found in verses 9–13. It is a church that is growing in truth and in love. There is sincere love between all the members. It hates evil and clings to what is good. People remark about the depth of fellowship and commitment between the Christians, because they are so devoted to each other in brotherly affection. It is a church where people honour one another, above themselves. They are not always looking to find fault, not always suspicious, because their habit of mind is to think the very best about other people. They are never lacking in zeal. The problem is perhaps cooling them down, rather than warming them up. It is a church which keeps its spiritual fervour, not just in spurts, but remains continually on fire for the Lord because it is a church that is consciously serving him; a church whose hope makes it joyful and whose patience endures affliction. It is characterized by faithful, believing prayer; a church where, if you are in need, people share with you because they love you, and a church whose homes are open, because its members practise hospitality.

'Lord, make my church a growing church and make me a growing Christian.'

7

Experiencing God Together

If you were called upon to quality test your Christian life, I wonder how you would go about it. What sort of standards would you apply? Would you be looking at the intensity of your feelings about God, or your experience of his love? Perhaps you would consider the duration of your prayers, or the amount of Bible study that you do? Or, would you rather test the quality of your Christian life by the number of activities in which you are involved, the good works you are committed to getting done? How would you test your Christian life? Well, the New Testament puts its emphasis elsewhere. The decisive test is very simple. Over and over again, it says you test the quality of your Christian life by how you get on with other Christians. That is the hallmark of reality, because it is the true index of our character, and it is character which counts with God. So as we come to study Paul's words in Colossians 3, remember that the exciting goals and challenges contained in this passage are not written as a manual for a life of detached saintliness.

Do not lie to each other, since you have taken off your old self with its practices and have put on the new self, which is being renewed in knowledge in the image of its Creator. Here there is no Greek or Jew, circumcised or uncircumcised, barbarian, Scythian, slave or free, but Christ is all, and is in all. Therefore, as God's chosen people, holy and dearly loved, clothe yourselves with compassion, kindness, humility, gentleness and patience. Bear with each other and forgive whatever grievances you may have against one another. Forgive as the Lord forgave you. And over all these virtues put on love, which binds them all together in perfect unity. Let the peace of Christ rule in your hearts, since as members of one body you were called to peace. And be thankful. Let the word of Christ dwell in you richly as you teach and admonish one another with all wisdom, and as you sing psalms, hymns and spiritual songs with gratitude in your hearts to God. And whatever you do, whether in word or deed, do it all in the name of the Lord Jesus, giving thanks to God the Father through him (Col 3:9-17).

These qualities are not to be cultivated in the quietness of our own rooms, away from everybody else. Paul's thought is never narrowly individual, or ingrown in that way. His concern is with our life together as a church, the body of Christ. The reason is that the universal church and every local company of Christians is designed by God to be a unique witness to the world, concerning the truth of the faith that we believe. She is designed to be the outpost of God's kingdom placed within this world, yet radically different from it. And the way in which the church demonstrates the difference is not by our gathering together on Sunday mornings, when other people may be in bed or doing the garden or washing the car; but by the quality of love between the people who are its members— a love that is real enough and great enough to overflow. That is the distinctive mark of Christian reality and it explains why it is the area that Satan attacks more than any other and why so many find it in practice to be so difficult.

But the fact that God has put us together in the body of Christ is one of his major means of making each of us more like Jesus. However young or old you may be, his passion is to develop the character of Jesus Christ in you. If you are a Christian he wants you to change, to grow increasingly like his Son. He never allows you to settle down in this world and say, 'Now, I have reached the satisfactory level of Christian discipleship, so I have no need to grow any more.' Always he wants us to be developing increasingly into the likeness of Christ and he does that by putting us together in the church, so that the New Testament pattern of life is not monasticism, but fellowship.

The first area of difference with which Paul deals in this passage is the new self (verse 10). No one drifts into becoming a Christian. There is a definite and radical change that has taken place in the life of everyone who is a true disciple of Christ. To use another biblical analogy, it is the same as becoming a citizen of another country. There is a new identity and a new loyalty involved. The old man, which is what the term here literally means, is put off, Paul says in verse 9, with all its practices. In contrast, the new self has been put on. That is one of his favourite ways of describing the experience of salvation or becoming a Christian.

You and I were born in solidarity with Adam, the head or fount of the human race. Like every other human being, we have all inherited Adam's sin; we were all born with a sinful nature. This old sinful self reveals its true colours through its rebellion against God. But when I turned to Jesus Christ and put my faith in him, I, like every Christian, put on the new self, because I became united to Christ who is the head of a new humanity. He is 'the last Adam' as Paul calls him in 1 Corinthians 15:45 and all those who are united to Jesus Christ by faith draw their spiritual life from him.

So for a Christian there has been a decisive change at the control centre of his life. He now declares that Jesus is Lord, which means that Jesus rules in his choices. Therefore, if Christ is the Head and we are the body, then individually and corporately we must produce in everyday terms a different kind of living. This is why Paul goes on to say in verse 10: you are 'being renewed in knowledge in the image of its Creator'. We could never do that on our own. We do not become Christians by trying to prove ourselves morally, or by going to church, or by doing good. We could not make ourselves like Jesus Christ even if we had a hundred lives to live, because there would always be that fatal flaw within us, which is our inherited sinful nature. But when we repent of our sin and open our lives to Christ, when he really becomes Lord in our experience, not only does he forgive the past, but he shares his divine life with us, and that is the eternal life of God implanted in our human personalities. We then have a new start, a new dynamic within us that begins to make us like Jesus.

But Paul emphasizes that it has to be developed because it is not delivered complete. You do not suddenly become perfect on conversion. But as the Creator of this new self is Christ, and we are being renewed in his image, so we are becoming more like him in our characters as we get to know him better. The personal encounter-knowledge of God deepens as we listen to him speaking to us in the Bible each day. As we do so, God's word comes into our minds and hearts and we begin to find our decisions are being shaped by God's perspectives. So discovering what the Bible teaches becomes increasingly important to us, because it is the means by which we get to know God better. The more closely acquainted we become and the closer we follow him, the more we grow like him.

Paul's special concern here is to show the uniqueness of this new quality of life that is available only in Christ. As he explains in verse 11: 'Here there is no Greek or Jew, circumcised or uncircumcised, barbarian, Scythian, slave or free, but Christ is all, and is in all.' In this verse he depicts some of the main divisions and hostilities that existed in the ancient world, and which still exist in one way or another today between those who are in Adam and those who are in Christ. Verse 11 describes divisions between people on the basis of nationality (Greek or Jew), on the basis of religion (circumcised or uncircumcised), on the basis of culture (barbarian or Scythian), and on the basis of class (slave or free). Paul teaches that sub-divisions are part of the old self, people separating from one another because they are of a different nationality, religion, culture or class. But in the new humanity in Christ, seen in the church, all these distinctions have come to an end. The old self-centred divisions no longer exist because Christ is all and is in all. The barriers between people are for ever broken down, not by conferences, not by revolutions, not by protest marches, but by Jesus Christ. When Christ is in you, if he is number one in your life, then there is a unity of life and purpose between you and God. This means that you are united together in your new self with all the other believers in the Lord Jesus. You are in his body, with all true Christians everywhere, and there are no barriers.

Nothing else in the world can achieve that. No amount of money, no secret society or club you can belong to can break down barriers between people as Jesus does. Christians know that wherever they travel in the world, there is an instant oneness with other Christians. Christ in his church is one new man, so that there is a new order of society which is the living witness to Christ's transforming power in the contemporary world. That is why biblical unity matters so much and it is why any divisions between Christians in the church are abhorrent to God and must be healed. If we do not live that out practically, we deny the gospel.

Then, secondly, in verses 12–14, Paul writes about what I want to describe as the new outfit. The new self needs a new wardrobe or, as Paul puts it in verse 12:

'clothe yourselves with compassion, kindness, humility, gentleness and patience.' We all know that something new to wear, a new look or a new hairstyle, can do wonders for our morale. It was Shakespeare who said, 'The apparel oft proclaims the man,' and that is true. Our appearance is usually the way we first communicate with other people. Therefore, the new self must wear new Christian clothes which are, Paul is saying, strikingly visible. If there is a new life in us it must demonstrate itself to other people. Whether or not we wear (or have!) a 'Sunday best' is irrelevant. God wants people who are dressed inside in the right clothing, so that they can worship him and make him known in the world.

The clothing that the new self must wear is described in verse 12. It is rooted in very specific practical terms. If, says Paul, you are really one of God's chosen people, then you are a holy person. It has nothing to do with being spiritually perfect, but means that you have been set apart to belong to God, as his special treasured possession, through what he has done for you and in you. You are someone whom he loves in living contact with him, so this will be the wardrobe in which you meet and relate to other people.

'Clothe yourselves with compassion,' or, more literally, with 'a heart of pity'. This means that as Christians we should have a pre-disposition to look favourably on other people. We should be willing always to give them the benefit of the doubt. We should at all times try to enter deeply into what their life is like for them, on the other side of the wall, and then move out towards them with as much understanding and practical, positive love and help, as we can give. The reason that we are to behave in this way is because that is what God has done for us. Our religion is founded on the incarnation of Jesus Christ, who came into this world and gave himself up on the cross for us all. If, says Paul, you too are a Christian, then that is the path you follow. You wear the clothing of compassion. If you do not, you cannot claim to be a disciple of Christ.

Next, Paul deals with the subject of kindness because that quality describes the sort of soil in the heart in which compassion flourishes. What poisons relationships between people is when we insist on our own rights, determined, at whatever cost, to have our way and demanding that we must be recognized. The sovereign antidote to all that is humility and, indeed, kindness and humility go together. It is the humble person who is kind because he has started to see himself as God sees him, not as he likes to imagine himself or with the image he likes to put on other people. He has, by contrast, allowed the searchlight of God's word to shine into his life and show him his own sin and failings. As a result, he begins to realize that he has no ground on which to be anything else but kind to other people. Supposing all you said about that person with whom you cannot get along was flashed up on a wall for everyone to read. Supposing in your home, church or work place, all the comments you have made about one another recently were put up on a noticeboard and became public property. Would anybody be embarrassed? But that record is in heaven. God both hears and knows. Yet even though this is the case, God forgives us when we repent. He will blot the record out. He will not flash it up, or keep a score of our wrongs. He wants it to be finished, forgotten and buried in the depths of the sea. That is the mercy and grace of God. Paul makes clear here that if that is the sort of God we worship, there can be no room for our petty arrogance and inflated pride. Be kind, be humble, for it is because of the Lord's mercy we are not consumed.

You must, says Paul, prove your Christianity by your gentleness and your patience. Perhaps we can best understand those last two words in verse 12 by thinking about opposites. The opposite of gentleness is rudeness or harshness, and the opposite of patience is resentment and revenge. Christians should be known to have long fuses. Too often they have to be labelled like fireworks: 'Light the blue touch-paper and retire immediately.' We must, Paul teaches, exhibit those characteristics as God's people. There is to be in us a consideration for other people, a willingness rather to be wronged than to slander others, a refusal to nurture bitterness or harbour resentment, because they are killers. Gentleness and long-suffering complete the Christian's wardrobe.

So Paul goes on to emphasize in verse 13—and I cannot stress this strongly enough—'Bear with each other and forgive whatever grievances you may have against one another. Forgive as the Lord forgave you.' Those are commands Paul makes very clear from the Lord. Paul does not say that we should wait around and hope that God will change our situation, but rather that we should take ourselves in hand and determine that with God's help this will be our attitude, that we will be forbearing, forgiving Christians. After all, there is no other sort of genuine discipleship. Any Christian testimony that is not demonstrated by forbearance and forgiveness is likely to be at best only skin deep and may be sheer hypocrisy. Paul here in effect tells every one of us, 'You must take the initiative. Do not wait for others. Forgive as the Lord forgave you.' If we look at how the Lord forgave people, we can see that it was without waiting for restitution. He forgave us totally, freely, without keeping a score of wrongs. When God forgives, he forgets, because his forgiveness is total. It is essential for us all to realize that if we will not forget we cannot have forgiven. Of course there are scars of old wounds, which may be with us till our dying day, and in a sense they cannot be forgotten, any more than scars in our flesh can be. But what the Bible is concerned about is the willingness to let go, to forgive so freely that, as an act of will, we chose never to bring the matter up again. So if we find that there are scores in our lives against some other Christian, any kind of bitterness or resentment, we need to beware because that is the root that can ultimately strangle our spiritual life. This is one more reason why we need to be on our knees, day by day, asking for God's mercy, until we can truly forgive. It is sin to be unwilling to forgive other Christians, and it can also very quickly become suicide, emotionally and spiritually.

All too often we imagine that the plea 'I can't do it' exonerates us from blame and even personal responsibility. But it is for this reason that God has given us his Holy Spirit. He knows we are unable to do it, but the Spirit is given to us in order that we might become like the Lord Jesus, who can do it. If we yield to Christ, he will enable us to do it. For love, according to verses 14, is the guarantee that all these other virtues will be in place. Love gives cohesion by producing a new depth of fellowship and uniting God's people in a common service to one another and to the world. It is love that binds us together. Furthermore, it is clear from verse 14 that God's standard is nothing less than 'perfect unity'. He does not want a mere patched up tolerance of one another, but a completeness, a perfection of unity among his people. Nothing less than the best will do for God.

I feel, as will many of you reading this, that some of us may need to burn some of our old clothes. Some of those attitudes that verse 8 talks about—such as anger, rage, malice and slander—are so unlike Jesus that we need to get those clothes out and burn them. You will not need them again, nor should you put them back in the drawer. Instead, put on the new clothes of love, compassion, kindness, humility, gentleness and patience.

You may feel, though, that it is all very well to be exhorted to do this, but how can it happen? The scriptures never exhort us without telling us how to carry it out. Paul gives the answer in verses 15–17, the last section. We can call this 'a new input': 'Let the peace of Christ rule in your hearts . . . Let the word of Christ dwell in you richly . . . do it all in the name of the Lord Jesus.'

Let us sum up what we have seen so far. Our common life in the body of Christ is a proving ground of our character and the encouragement to live differently. As we put on the new clothes that Christ has provided we must let Christ's peace rule. The word 'rule' means 'to act as umpire', to call out the decisions like a referee in a game or a judge at a sports contest. The reference here is corporate, not to a sort of inner peace I may have as an individual. That can so easily be self-delusion. It is the peace we all experience as part of the body of Christ, or, to put it another way, peaceful coexistence. Paul teaches that the harmony of the church is God's will for his people and he has provided Christ's peace in order to allow that to happen. Therefore, Christ must rule and settle any dispute and the mark of the happening will be that the peace of Christ 'calls out the decisions' in all our hearts. We are not to be spiritual prima donnas, disputing every decision and constantly objecting to what the umpire says. 'Let the peace of Christ rule.' If you are the sort of Christian who ought really to have a notice round your neck saying, 'Danger—high explosive,' or, 'Beware of the dog,' something is wrong with your Christianity.

The peace of Christ is a kingdom where a believer is protected as long as he seeks the will of the king and is obedient to the Head of the body. Christ will do that for us, says Paul, if we let him. In the same way as the umpire at the tennis match will run the match for you if you will let him (and if you are a good sportsman you will) so if you are a good Christian you will let the peace of Christ be authoritative in your relationships within his body. Christians who live in and contribute to Christ's revolutionary new community like that are full of thankfulness (verse 15b) because they are experiencing a taste of heaven on earth. Where Christ's rule is accepted there will be love and peace, so we shall want to praise him for that. If our experience of thanksgiving in corporate worship is to be deep and genuine, it must flow from right attitudes to God and to our fellow worshippers. That is essential if what we do together in worship is to have spiritual authenticity.

That leads us to Paul's second input: 'Let the word of Christ dwell in you richly' (verse 16). By this he means that you should allow Christ's word to be so much at home that you are enriched by it in every area of life and experience. After all, all genuine spiritual progress and all authentic worship are at base a response to God's truth. The analogy is one which is drawn from our experience of giving hospitality. When someone comes to our home, as a guest, we try to give them pleasant food, to provide them with a warm bed and comfortable room, if they stay. We do not shut them up in the attic and put them on a starvation diet. But what do you do with the word of God in your life? Some of us effectively put it in the spare room and mark it 'Sundays only', excusing ourselves on the grounds that the business world is too difficult to live in by the Bible's standards. Or do you entertain God richly in every part of your life? Does he have full run of your house, so that each area of your life is under the authority of the word of Christ? Only those who are under the word will have the necessary wisdom to teach and admonish one another, as verse 16 says, and yet we all have a responsibility to fulfil for the well-being of one another in Christ. Faithfulness and thankfulness for the word are seen in our response to it, by obeying what God says and by praising him for who he is and what he has done for us.

Paul tells us here that healthy Christians are singing Christians. Because gratitude is at the heart of our worship, that is why the content of what we sing is so important, whether we use words of Scripture like Psalms, or traditional hymns or contemporary spiritual songs. There is a place for each but they must be based on the word of Christ and therefore scriptural in content, because if they are not, they cannot be worthy worship. All worship must be Christ-centred. True worship celebrates the mighty acts of God. Rather than focusing on what I feel like as the worshipper, it focuses on God, the object of my adoration, on who he is and on what he has done for me. Worship abases itself before God and says firstly, 'God be merciful to me, a sinner,' and then, secondly, assured of forgiveness and cleansing, 'Now I want to praise you with all my heart and to live a life that is as much like Jesus as you can make it.'

That sort of worship cannot be contained in a couple of hours on a Sunday. For verse 17 says, 'Whatever you do, whether in word or deed, do it all in the name of the Lord Jesus, giving thanks to God the Father through him.' That is where we began, and it remains the ultimate test—the name of Jesus. It is not a magic formula tacked on to our own enterprises, like a stamp of approval. Nor is it a conventional way of signing off before we say 'Amen' at the end of our prayers. What Paul is saying is that our whole lives are to be under the authority of that name. We belong to him, so that no words that we speak, no actions we perform, should be the sort of words or actions that could not be done in Christ's name and therefore in praise to God the Father. That is the test, the test of reality as we experience God together.

These standards are very demanding and as I reflect on them they bring me to recognize how much further I, at any rate, have to travel in the school of discipleship. I can identify more deeply than ever with those other words of Paul, expressing his resolve, in the midst of his short-fall: 'Not that I have already obtained all this, or have already been made perfect, but I press on to take hold of that for which Christ Jesus took hold of me' (Phil 3:12). The exciting thing is that we are not alone in this pilgrimage.

We can help one another forward as we experience God more deeply together, with the result that we enjoy him more completely in our fellowship than we ever could in isolation.

8

A Heart for Service

As we come to the subject of ministry in the church, we focus on a short but graphic passage from Luke's gospel. The context is that the disciples are in the upper room on the night on which Jesus is to be betrayed, on the Thursday evening before his death on Good Friday. He has just instituted what we call the Lord's Supper.

> Also a dispute arose among them as to which of them was considered to be greatest. Jesus said to them, 'The kings of the Gentiles lord it over them; and those who exercise authority over them call themselves Benefactors. But you are not to be like that. Instead, the greatest among you should be like the youngest, and the one who rules like the one who serves. For who is greater, the one who is at the table or the one who serves? Is it not the one who is at the table? But I am among you as one who serves. You are those who have stood by me in my trials. And I confer on you a kingdom, just as my Father conferred one on me, so that you may eat and drink at my table in my kingdom and sit on thrones, judging the twelve tribes of Israel' (Lk 22:24–30).

In this book so far we have concentrated on the priorities that we seek as the church of Jesus Christ and therefore the goals that the Bible sets for us as God's people. Those two priorities are firstly that we are growing like the Lord Jesus and then to express that in our relationships with one another. We are to be active in support and in encouraging one another, in the body of Christ, as we build each other up in that Christlikeness.

In this chapter and the next we will study the function of leadership in the church. Over the centuries, the church has developed various hierarchies in leadership. If you look around the church of Jesus Christ in our own country, and indeed across the world, you will find a great variety of structures within local church congregations. Sometimes the church seems to have modelled itself upon the army. In such churches there is a hierarchy of office, a pyramid structure of command. Orders, advice or direction are handed down from the top. In other cases the church has patterned itself more on the business world, and most of the very large churches across the world have to be run like corporations. In some churches, democracy has become a sacred principle, so that all forward movement has to be approved by the entire congregation. In such cases, leadership is often stifled and progress reduced to a snail's pace. Each of these patterns has biblical ingredients and can be shown to have certain strengths, but none is complete in itself and each has inherent weaknesses. We may learn from secular models, but must not accept them uncritically, any more than we would model our understanding of the lordship of Christ on earthly kingship, or the kingdom of God upon modern democratic states.

We need some radical biblical thinking when we come to consider ministry in the church, for there are biblical distinctives which must be applied if the church is to be true to her Head, her origin and her purpose. All of us are conditioned by the world in which we live, by the society in which we have grown up and by the churches of which we have been a part. The radical thinking that Jesus brings to us, as we begin to consider this concept, is raised by the question that the disciples were debating in the upper room: who are the greatest in the kingdom of heaven? This is a question about the nature of spiritual greatness, and if we find out who the greatest are, should we want to be among them? Or is that unsanctified ambition? What is God looking for in our lives? What is the bottom line of Christian service?

That may seem to apply especially to the leaders within the church, but it actually applies to all of us who have any sort of involvement in the body of Christ, whether as leaders or followers. As we have seen, every Christian has a unique part to play and as each part works properly, it contributes to the building up of the whole body. In that very real sense, every Christian is in the ministry, because every Christian has works of service to which God has called him or her. The New Testament knows nothing about a special separate caste of Christian who is a full-time professional, called to do all the work. Rather it teaches that we are all in the body of Christ together. While it is perfectly legitimate, therefore, for local churches to set aside men and women to serve full-time in the church, that does not make them into a priestly caste, or confer on them a clergy status which is separated from the laity. We are *one* body; we all have different functions, but we are all involved in the ministry to which God has called us as his people.

These are the questions this passage centres on. Luke alone among the gospel writers tells us that there was strife, or a dispute, in the upper room. Jesus had just instituted the Lord's supper. He had taken the old Passover meal and transformed it, by referring it to his passion and his imminent death. The shadow of the cross was growing longer every minute over the Lord and the disciples, and it was at that moment, Luke tells us in chapter 22, verse 24, that a dispute arose among them as to which of them was considered to be the greatest. In both Matthew's and

Mark's Gospels we have similar passages at other times, indicating that this was a recurring theme among the disciples. They were very interested to know who was the greatest, and it is my observation that it is still a recurring theme, sometimes to the point of obsession, among Christian disciples today. All sorts of Christian groups are beset by what can only be described as power struggles; torn by people who are seeking to be, according to their understanding, among the greatest in that group.

John tells us that as they went into that upper room, none of the disciples was willing to perform the service function of washing the others' feet. Water and a towel were there, but none of them would do it. It was a menial task and as they were considering which of them were likely to have key positions in the 'cabinet' when the kingdom came, none of them was willing to be caught washing the others' feet and seeming to be less than great. So of course, as John 13 tells us, Jesus rose from the meal and very pointedly and very deliberately took the water and the towel and did the job of washing the disciples' feet himself.

That unwillingness to serve on the disciples' part presupposes the attitude which Luke records here as a quarrel, for that was what it was. Furthermore, it is essential to notice the extraordinary context in which it took place. We regard the communion service as a very important aspect of our corporate worship. We would be horrified if, as we came to a communion service, we found members of the church disputing, arguing, striving with one another over who was the greatest. But when Jesus instituted this remembrance service, that is precisely what was happening. As he approached the cross, the disciples were a million miles away in spirit. Evidently they thought the kingdom was about to be established. Jesus had just said, in Luke 22:18, 'I tell you I will not drink again of the fruit of the vine until the kingdom of God comes.' So they took that to mean it was imminent. Jesus was about to take power and to reign: hence their dispute about occupying the top positions. They seem to have had no idea about the true nature of the inauguration of the kingdom of God. They also possessed very little concept at all that the king was going to reign from a cross, on which he would be lifted up for their sins, or that his kingdom was radically different from any other kingdom the world had ever seen.

It is also probable that the traditional style of celebrating the Passover contributed to their simmering jealousies and smouldering disagreements. The seating arrangements were something that every host at a Passover meal thought about very carefully. Usually, they sat around the three sides of a square, and in the centre of the middle or top table was the host, who would, of course, be Jesus, as the leader of the group. It was traditional that on the right hand of the host sat either the senior member of the family or the most honoured guest, on his left hand the second most honoured guest, and on his second right the third most honoured guest, and so on round the table. One can see this in Jesus' parable earlier in Luke about the man who went to the wedding feast and sat at the end of the table. There he was told, 'Friend, move up to a better place. You ought to be recognized as an honoured guest' (see Lk 14:8-11). On this occasion, we know that John was next to Jesus, because he tells us as much in John 13:23. So they began asking if that meant he would be the top man in the kingdom as well.

I believe that the gospels record this faithfully to show us just how self-conscious, how self-centred and status-seeking the disciples were, even at this moment. There is still a temptation for Christians to use any position of trust or leadership, any gifts that God has given us for our own kudos and ambition, for building up our image of ourselves. Why else do Christians want to hold on to office or to the titles they may have in the church of Jesus Christ? It is so easy for us to love pre-eminence. If we do not have it, we want it and are never tempted to give it up if we do. But Jesus Christ dealt with that sort of attitude ruthlessly and immediately.

He taught them three things. The first is a grave danger, which is explained in Luke 22:25, 26. Jesus said to them, 'The kings of the Gentiles lord it over them; and those who exercise authority over them call themselves Benefactors. But you are not to be like that.' In the original, it says, 'But you, not so.' Jesus here identifies this attitude of the disciples as totally foreign to his kingdom. Instead it belongs to this world, that of the Gentiles, or secular society. For an attitude of self-seeking in the church and using ministry gifts and responsibilities to serve me rather than others is a thoroughly pagan one. This was the root of their problem, and it still lies at the root of much strife and disagreement among Christians today. They were thinking about the kingdom or, to put it another way, about the church and the affairs of Christ, with a worldly mind, because they had become infected by the prevailing attitude of the people around them. They had begun to identify greatness with position and power, with privilege and prestige. But Jesus says that that is a thoroughly pagan way of looking at things. To identify greatness by externals is heathen, and to be concerned about one's own status is an unworthy concept for a Christian.

The worldly men, the kings of the Gentiles, get themselves called Benefactors. While they claim that they are doing good for others, in fact, says Jesus, they are really living for themselves. The kings of Egypt, for example, took that title. The more these rulers milked their people by their taxes, the more they were called Benefactors—at least by themselves! You have only to read almost any contemporary politician's election address to see that things have not changed so much in 2,000 years. They also get themselves called Benefactors and will tell you at election times what great ones they have been. Although that may hide a sinister exploitation of people, it is still a thoroughly worldly way of behaviour. The main point that the Lord is making here is that external assessment and all the outward trappings of pomp and show which have so often infected the church are unworthy of his disciples. Man looks on the outward appearance, God looks at the heart. That, of course, is why we should never judge one another, because you cannot see my heart, nor I yours. We are therefore not to judge one another but to love and care for one another. For immediately we start judging from outward appearance, we become Gentile and not Christian.

The Christian attitude, says Jesus, in verse 26, is in sharp contrast to that. While we can perhaps understand the disciples, at that point in time, with their vision of an earthly kingdom, which they thought was going to come in at any moment, we cannot sit back complacently and assume that we are immune from this. Sadly, this very kind of worldliness still permeates many Christians and many churches. Let me explain what I mean. Of course, we know as Christians that we cannot earn our status before God. We are not performing good works so that we will be acceptable to him, because we know that we could never ever reach God by our own efforts. One sin would be enough to cast us out of his presence. We have to be forgiven; we have to be reconciled and accepted by God, entirely on the grounds of his grace toward us, in the Lord Jesus Christ. So all of us who are Christians rejoice in the gift of God's love. We praise him for the forgiveness that he has granted us and we recognize that it is just that—a free gift. It is unmerited, unearned, and undeserved.

But, as Christians we live in a world that operates in a totally different way. We live in an environment dominated by status systems and achievement goals. So it becomes quite natural for us as Christians in the 1980s to be squeezed easily and unthinkingly into the world's value system. We accept its way of doing things in the church, assuming all the time that Christian greatness is measured by the world's yardstick of outward success, position or authority. But that, Jesus makes clear, is only an external assessment and God judges the heart. Our external evaluations can be utterly wrong, yet how easily we fall into them. Our thinking gets so twisted that we even take God's means of grace and make them into status symbols of Christian growth. This then becomes the yardstick by which we can criticize or assess other people.

The danger is that as Christians we set up our own standards of authority and greatness or, for that matter, shape our own criteria of service, in which of course we manage to come off best. It is as though we had been tempted into saying, 'Yes, I know I'm saved only by the grace of God, and it's through faith in the Lord Jesus that my salvation has been received. But, of course, now I have to prove that by going on working my way up the particular spiritual ladder that I'm climbing, in order to show how mature I am as a Christian.' It is a very subtle danger that we climb an invisible ladder, by which we exalt ourselves and start to lord it over others. We set up our ladders as criteria of what it means to be a keen Christian, but we are really giving our lives to a subtle heresy; that having been saved by grace, we now can only be accepted by our own effort. Unless we are very careful, that can lead to a frustrating and ultimately negative doctrine of sanctification by works.

For example, how do we know what a mature or maturing Christian is? What is greatness? What is spiritual perception and quality? Think of the ladders we climb by which to attain to spiritual eminence. Some of us assess spiritual maturity by the things we do, the number and type of good works to which we are committed and it is all too easy, if that is your particular ladder, to think, 'I'm doing much more than other people, so I must be higher up the ladder than they are. I deserve to be recognized for my high rungmanship. I am a great Christian.' Or, it may be the things we do *not* do, the negatives that are being cut out of our lives; surely if those things have gone, it must mean I am nearer to the Lord than my brother is, or than I was before? Or the ladder may be our intellectual understanding of the faith; because I understand it better than others, I think of myself as a little further up the ladder than they are. I look at my knowledge as something right in my life. It can be the Christian books that I have on my shelf or even perhaps that I read! Equally, for others it is marked by the books they would never read. It can be the gifts that we received or the verses that we have memorized. It can be the experience of God's blessings that we have enjoyed or sacrifices that we make. It can be the number of years we have been a member of the church or served in a particular capacity.

All of these can be means by which we establish in our own mind our own relative greatness, though we would never put it in such terms. We are able to lord it over other people just a little bit, because we have climbed higher up the ladder than they have. To all this Jesus says, 'Not so with you. That is not the way in which my kingdom works.' This extended image of ladder-climbing is not original to me. I discovered it in Keith Miller's little-known but extremely perceptive and challenging book *The Becomers* (Hodder & Stoughton, 1973). In that book he describes how fatally easy it is for a keen and active Christian to be launched onto a conveyor belt which takes him from regular Sunday church attendance through teaching in Sunday School, singing in the choir, being a steward, leading an organization of the church, right on to being senior deacon or elder and ultimately into the ordained ministry. Irrespective of whether or not his life and witness as a layman might be more fulfilling, he is parcelled up and sent off to theological college. And when he is qualified, what does he discover but a whole new set of ministerial ladders to climb. Imagine the scene a few years later, at a gathering of ministers, when an old classmate walks up to him. Keith Miller writes:

> 'Where are you serving now, George?' he says with a concerned look. (It is interesting to note that this question is almost always asked by a man in a large or prestigious church.)
>
> Old George stammers, 'Arp, Texas.'
>
> 'Oh, yes, *Arp*. How many people do you have there now (in your congregation)?'
>
> 'Seventy' (including three dogs in the yard and a couple of neighbour kids who play on the property during the service).
>
> 'Umm, well, I'm sure that's a great place to get *experience*.' And he proceeds to tell poor old George about his thriving and growing parish. This is called 'rung-dropping' and it tells the other person that he is lower than you on the ladder.

Yet Jesus says, 'Not so, with you.' The world is full of 'rung-dropping'. All around us people are continually putting other people down. Everybody has their ladder, which they climb with the purpose of demonstrating that you are lower down than they are. But the radical difference that being a Christian makes, Jesus says, is that you do not live that way because you do not need that sort of security. The disciple's security is in Christ. You are liberated from pacing yourself against somebody else, or seeing how high you are on the ladder. I wish that as Christians we would recognize that, chop up our ladders and burn them for ever, realizing that it is in Christ alone that our true security is found. We are not continually having to prove to ourselves where we stand, even with regard to one another, because we are *all* in the 'serving' ministry. Do not misunderstand my point here. Many of the things I have mentioned are right and good, expressions of true Christian faith even, but none of them is a measure of Christian greatness. Not one of these things earns you righteousness or privilege or power, even if your motivation is 100% pure. The great danger is that we develop the world's view, busily climbing our ladder, quietly judging and dismissing other Christians who, we think, are lower down, or even in their folly climbing the wrong ladder, which is much worse! And Jesus says, 'No, that is worldliness. That denies my gospel and there is no place for that sort of status in the Christian community— none at all.'

Secondly, the positive side, Jesus shows us a great principle. Look at verses 26b and 27a: 'Instead, the greatest among you should be like the youngest, and the one who rules like the one who serves. For who is greater, the one who is at the table or the one who serves?' We can see how our Lord's teaching here utterly reverses those worldly values, which we so easily imbibe. He does not say, 'Now I want you to understand that there are no great ones in my kingdom.' Nor does he teach, 'I want you to realize that all ambition is wrong.' He does not condemn us to be mediocre; indeed, the opposite is true. God wants us to fulfil our personal potential, to be somebody, which is why his Son died to redeem us and the reason why he brought us into a relationship with himself. He really wants us to count for him in the world. He desires that our lives should be enriched by his development of all the gifts that he has given us. He wants us to be complete as people. But, he gives us criteria and standards by which to achieve this that are totally different from those of the world.

One foundation principle that comes out very clearly here is that if you want to fulfil your potential as a Christian, you will achieve it by serving. In the ancient world, age conferred privilege, and to be the youngest was to be the lowliest. This, says Jesus, is true Christian greatness. This is what leadership in ministry is all about, what Christian work entails. It is given into the hands of a servant. The Lord Jesus has already given us a striking example of this by washing the disciples' feet, and he now presses it home with an illustration taken from the meal table, the very place where they were sitting. He asks in verse 27, 'who is greater, the one who is at the table or the one who serves?' Naturally the diner, the one who sits at the table, is esteemed higher than the waiter. The verb here *diakoneo*, 'to serve at table', was a word used to indicate any form of holy service. One would naturally expect Jesus to be in the supreme place, as the Lord, and to be waited on by others. But read the staggering words that he speaks at the end of verse 27: 'But I am among you as one who serves.' That is the great principle. 'I, the Lord of Glory, the eternal Son of God, the Creator and Sustainer of everything, the Saviour of the world, the Judge of all men, I,' Jesus is saying, 'am among you as a servant, a waiter. And in doing all this, I am enacting a parable of what it means to be a member of the kingdom of heaven. The truly great, the benefactor, in my kingdom is the servant of all.' That is one of the most staggering sentences and one of the most penetrating challenges in the whole of the New Testament. We need to meditate on it, hard and long.

'I am among you as one who serves.' That one sentence expresses the controlling principle of Christ's life and ministry on earth. Always, he was the Servant King. Not once was his power used gratuitously to minister to himself. Right at the beginning of his ministry he had won that battle, during the forty days of temptation in the desert, refusing to turn stones into bread or to throw himself from the highest point of the temple. He would not minister to himself. He was supremely to be the man for others. So, how are his subjects to use the delegated authority he has conferred upon them in his body, the church? The King's life provides the model. The church, unique among human organizations, exists for those who are not yet its members. Members of the body are committed to the life of self-sacrifice that they have seen exemplified in their Head. The supreme example of the principle in practice is seen in the ministry of Jesus. As we put other Gospel passages alongside this one, the Holy Spirit fills out our understanding of what such ministry entails.

For example, there is a parallel passage in Mark 10: 42–45:

> Jesus called them together and said, 'You know that those who are regarded as rulers of the Gentiles lord it over them, and their high officials exercise authority over them. Not so with you. Instead, whoever wants to become great among you must be your servant, and whoever wants to be first must be slave of all. For even the Son of Man did not come to be served, but to serve, and to give his life as a ransom for many.'

To be a servant means constantly to be giving, Jesus is saying, even to the ultimate point of self-sacrifice. Indeed, he defines that self-giving as the central purpose of his coming. The Servant King came to suffer to give his life as a ransom. Clearly, that is Christ's unique work, but at the same time it is also the pattern of all discipleship ministry, all true work for the kingdom of God. While we can never give our lives as a ransom for anyone, yet we are to follow the Saviour's example by giving ourselves away in his service, however costly. That service is directed outwards to our suffering, broken world.

I like the story of the service station (an apt name) in the USA that was advertising on its forecourt, 'We will crawl under your car oftener and get ourselves dirtier than any of our competitors.' We should be able to put the equivalent claim on every church notice board in the country. Our vision is directed outwards to the 'many', who do not yet know Christ. They are to be the focus of our ministry. But, sadly, in so many churches most of the energy output is directed to carrying Christians, who anyway ought to be drawing their resources from Christ personally. Isn't that why so many Christians find church life so frustrating? We prevent ourselves from finding the Lord's fulfilment in serving the world of need, by becoming introspective and self-centred, always quality-testing our subjective experiences of fellowship and worship, usually with negative results. We get caught up in arguments about who is really in charge and petty-minded power struggles. We start to judge and criticize our fellow Christians, often merely to hold on to our little bit of imagined status, or to carve out our pathetic little empires. How do you think the Servant Lord regards all that? I think it breaks his heart. It should break ours too, because it is not what other people think of us that matters, but what Jesus thinks. That is where freedom is to be found. The rest is bondage.

Another similar passage is found in Luke 9:46–48:

> An argument started among the disciples as to which of them would be the greatest. Jesus, knowing their thoughts, took a little child and had him stand beside him. Then he said to them, 'Whoever welcomes this little child in my name welcomes me; and whoever welcomes me welcomes the one who sent me. For he who is least among you all—he is the greatest.'

Again, Jesus directs the disciples away from thoughts of personal ambition, to humble service. Instead of coveting position or power, we are to be concerned about the weak and dependent, symbolized by the little child, and to receive them. This implies a love that protects, cares and serves. That, says Jesus, is spiritual greatness. A contemporary Jewish scholar has made the point that while the

rabbis never wearied of preaching humility and its greatness, Jesus introduced a totally new dimension into the
discussion, that of humility with service. That concept
was his special characteristic.

Let us go back to John's account of the upper room for a
moment, after Jesus has completed the foot-washing:

> 'Do you understand what I have done for you?' he asked
> them. 'You call me "Teacher" and "Lord", and rightly so, for
> that is what I am. Now that I, your Lord and Teacher, have
> washed your feet, you also should wash one another's feet. I
> have set you an example that you should do as I have done for
> you. I tell you the truth, no servant is greater than his master,
> nor is a messenger greater than the one who sent him. Now
> that you know these things, you will be blessed if you do
> them' (Jn 13:12-17).

As far as the life of Christian discipleship is concerned,
happiness is action-shaped. In his discerning, penetrating
way, the Servant King puts his finger on our problem. It is
one thing to know these things, but quite another to do
them. Yet this is our calling. Christian discipleship is a life
of foot-washing, meeting the needs of others, however
unpleasant or inconvenient that might appear to be.
Ministry is commitment to love and care and to be
involved at the point of others' needs, irrespective of the
cost. That is how we serve one another within the body of
Christ, and it is how the body serves the world.

'I am among you as one who serves.' What does that
mean for us today? So many Christians stand the thing on
its head. They pretend that Jesus is saying, 'If you want to
be great in my kingdom, you must prove yourself first in a
lowly place of insignificance and then, gradually, you will
be promoted.' But that sort of ladder-climbing is precisely
what he is not saying. The message of Jesus is that faithful
service, however lowly it may appear on the human value-
scale, is in itself true spiritual greatness. So do not let the

world condition you with its false values and distorted goals. Take up the task God is calling you to fulfil and trust him for the grace to do it. Persevere with what God has given you to do, even if it is costly and you often feel weary, or hurt, or very much alone. 'It is the way the master went. Should not the servant tread it still?'

Don't give up loving and praying for those in your family who mock your faith and give you a rough ride, because their minds are blind to spiritual realities. Keep serving at work, even though you are put upon, and they take all sorts of advantages, because you are conscientious. Don't despair if you feel cut off and neglected because you are bringing up toddlers at home and all your time has to be devoted to their needs, or to the daily treks between home and the school gate. It is the Master's work you are doing and he always gives more grace. 'Whatever you do, work at it with all your heart, as working for the Lord, not for men, since you know you will receive an inheritance from the Lord as a reward. It is the Lord Christ you are serving' (Col 3:23, 24). As you serve, with your eyes on Jesus, you will find that there is neither the time nor the inclination to be looking over your shoulder at other Christians and trying to compare or assess yourself against them. Spiritual greatness is not outward at all. It consists of a heart like the Master's—a servant heart, a heart of love.

When you grow weary and the cost seems too great, remember how the passage ends. The party is coming. The banquet will be prepared and one day those who have been faithful waiters at others' tables will sit, eat and drink, with Jesus, at his. The kingdom *will* come in all its fulness, and then faithfulness will not go unrewarded. But for now, it is the serving that counts.

9

A Matter of Discipline

Tolerance is widely applauded as one of the most popular virtues of our day. Ironically, the only attitude that we may validly refuse to tolerate is other people's intolerance. It is when Christians start to affirm that Jesus is the *only* way to God, that they run into trouble and face charges of extremism and intolerant absolutism. As long as Jesus is kept as one of the many options on the shelves of the religious supermarket, there will be no difficulties or opposition.

In every generation, the biggest threat the church faces is the prevailing secular culture, which will attempt to squeeze the citizens of heaven into conformity with the shapes and patterns of this world. The twin dangers are that the church either meekly succumbs or she over-reacts to unbiblical extremes, so as to define her distinctiveness over against the secular culture, in such a way that the truth is distorted by over-correction. We must always be looking for the biblical perpendicular which is the only way to steady the swing of the pendulum. Today, tolerance seems to have produced a 'rubber spine' attitude in many churches, with regard to both doctrine and behaviour. An outside observer of some churches might well ask what has to be believed today as an irreducible minimum for Christian orthodoxy. Are the words 'heresy' or 'error' now so redundant that anything can be accepted as a fresh 'interpretation' of Christian truth? Does the Creed still constitute the church? Similarly, in the area of personal behaviour, are there any actions or attitudes that are always morally wrong? Or have situation ethics developed to such a point that repentance is no longer meaningful, except for the sin of intolerance? Is there still a place for church discipline?

It is hardly surprising that in some circles equivalent over-reaction has been gaining ground. 'Accountability' has become a popular theme. It is certainly a biblical concept but it has sometimes been used to describe a heavy-handed dominance by Christian leaders over the lives of their flock, and the imposition of man-made rules that must be adhered to in detail, far beyond the teaching of Scripture, thus removing the right of private judgement from the individual Christian and instituting a new legalism. So where is the biblical perpendicular?

It is no new problem. The church at Corinth was facing the same kind of pressure from the unbelieving world. Although the details may differ, the principles for dealing with them remain the same and they form the substance of Paul's first letter to that church. Full of practical instruction, but always founded in theological principles, it is a model of how the apostles taught the Christian doctrines. Theirs was not the abstract approach of systematized textbooks. Rather, they took the real practical problems the churches were facing and applied God's revealed truth to life.

In Corinth there were doctrinal pressures that centred around the ideas of wisdom and power, so prevalent in the culture. There were scores of secret religions, and sects, each with their travelling philosophers, peddling their own special revelations of wisdom, to confer salvation.

The church was tempted to want a message that was intellectually fashionable, to compete on equal terms with secular philosophies. They wanted preachers, skilled in rhetoric, who would compel conviction in the sheer brilliance of their arguments and the impressiveness of their verbal fireworks.

Paul saw in this a threat to the gospel itself. It is as though the twentieth century church were to put all its efforts into producing brilliant television celebrities, ready to compromise what they said for the popularity and success of their performance. So Paul addresses himself to the question, 'What is Christian wisdom', especially in chapters 1–4. Allied to this is the question, 'What is Christian freedom?' in chapters 5–11. If the gospel sets us free from the Old Testament law, then are we free to do as we like? If we are no longer bound by Jewish food restrictions, does that equally extend to other areas of life, such as sexual relationships? What bearing does our behaviour in the body have on our personal identity in Christ and our eternal destiny? In a society well-provided with a multiplicity of gods, temples and sacrifices, the issue was how far to confront the culture and where, if at all, there was room for compromise or tolerance.

The relevance of such questions to church life today hardly needs comment. We are going to look at one representative passage in which Paul confronts a moral problem, which was infecting the church and draining its spiritual life and energy. In so doing, we can learn a great deal about the principles of discipline within the church, an ingredient which is much needed today, but is often not only lacking but actively resisted in church life. The fact that Paul deals with a matter of personal morality in the context of a church letter is in itself a powerful reminder of the corporate context of all our acts as Christians. How each individual Christian behaves has its impact on the whole body, and the whole church has a responsibility for the right conduct of its individual members. That is the thrust of 1 Corinthians 5.

> It is actually reported that there is sexual immorality among you, and of a kind that does not occur even among pagans: A man has his father's wife. And you are proud! Shouldn't you rather have been filled with grief and have put out of your fellowship the man who did this? Even though I am not physically present, I am with you in spirit. And I have already passed judgment on the one who did this, just as if I were present. When you are assembled in the name of our Lord Jesus and I am with you in spirit, and the power of our Lord Jesus is present, hand this man over to Satan, so that the sinful nature may be destroyed and his spirit saved on the day of the Lord. Your boasting is not good. Don't you know that a little yeast works through the whole batch of dough? Get rid of the old yeast that you may be a new batch without yeast—as you really are. For Christ, our Passover Lamb, has been sacrificed. Therefore let us keep the Festival, not with the old yeast, the yeast of malice and wickedness, but with bread without yeast, the bread of sincerity and truth (1 Cor 5:1–8).

It is the whole church that is chided by Paul, for not taking action against such a flagrant case of immorality. By such neglect, the church's witness among the pagans has inevitably been compromised and discredited. Every local fellowship of Christians is representative of Jesus Christ. We cannot avoid being witnesses—either for, or against him. That is why Christ's standards must be upheld by the church, through its leaders, and why discipline must be exercised against its unrepentant offenders. The fact that such things are unpopular today does not make them any less necessary. Too many Christians imagine they have freedom to do whatever they like and still remain as members of Christ's body; but that is licence, not liberty. Unless there is an exercise of discipline within the local body of Christ, we fail in love, both to our Lord and to one another. Of course, the exercise of discipline today is

made the more difficult by our multiplicity of denominations and local church options. A Christian who is disciplined in one fellowship can very easily walk out, rather
than repent, and walk straight into another local church,
without facing up to the issue involved or revealing any of
the problems in the new congregation. This is a powerful
reason why it is important for the local churches to live in
fellowship with one another and to keep open communication between their leaders, so that these easy options,
which are ultimately spiritually destructive, may be closed
off.

As saints, we need discipline. The particular case mentioned in verse 1 is regarded as incest in the law of God:
'Do not have sexual relations with your father's wife' (Lev
18:8). Such a thing was condemned even by pagans, as
notoriously loose in sexual matters as life in Corinth was.
It seems likely, therefore, that this man's sin may well
have been justified in the church by spurious spiritual
reasoning. We have been set free from the Old Testament
law, it was argued. Our spirits are eternally alive in Christ,
so it does not really matter what we do with our bodies.
Perhaps there was some disagreement within the congregation as to how to deal with this situation, but the fact
was that the church has done nothing about it and so they
were effectively overlooking such a gross moral lapse. It
had become a scandal against the name of Christ in
Corinth. And this was the church that boasted about their
superior spirituality. How blind and foolish they were!
Later in the letter (12:26) Paul will be teaching them that
the church is not just a collection of individuals, but a
living body: 'If one part suffers, every part suffers with it'.
By the same analogy, when a man brings shame on the
name of Jesus, it is not just himself but the whole church
that suffers. Paul had looked in vain for the reaction of
shame characterized by godly sorrow and followed by
separation. Instead he found only pride. In our western

individualism, we find it hard to accept this as a spiritual reality, yet everywhere the Bible assumes it. Every sin that a Christian commits wounds the body. Every unkind word, every unloving action, every broken relationship, every good that is not done, affects the whole. We do not stand alone in isolation and that is why the church has to exercise discipline over its membership.

Verses 3–5 provide Paul's remedy for the situation. First, he establishes that there is no doubt about the guilt of the individuals. Of course, that point has to be made before any effective discipline can be exercised. So he begins by sweeping away any of the specious arguments that might have been advanced in support of this man. His action is a crime against God and against man and the apostle has already judged it as such. That is a responsibility of godly leadership. Had Paul been challenged on this and asked, 'Who are you to condemn someone else?', his answer would undoubtedly have been, 'I am a man whose conscience is captive to the word of God.' This is what it means to live under the absolute authority of God's truth. There is no way round the situation; sin is sin. It is not a matter of personality differences or a power complex on Paul's part. He is using scripture to pass judgement, because the church has failed to fulfil its biblical responsibility.

But then in verse 4 he prescribes the action which is to be taken. The church must gather together, and as they do so they can be sure not only of Paul's spiritual support but, far more importantly, the presence and power of the Lord Jesus. He had himself promised, 'where two or three come together in my name, there am I with them' (Mt 18:20). It is significant that the context of that promise given by Jesus to the disciples is one of church discipline. The church gathers to exercise specific disciplinary action against the offending member (verse 5). While the precise meaning of 'hand this man over to Satan' is difficult to establish, it seems to mean expulsion from the church (see verses 2b and 13). Outside the church is the sphere of Satan and the immoral man must be consigned to that by a solemn action of the congregation. His membership is forfeited, but it is important to underline the purpose of the disciplinary action. Paul stresses this is not a punishment for sin but as a means by which the offender can be spiritually restored. There may well be severe physical consequences. The Bible clearly teaches that Satan is allowed on occasions to cause sickness, such as with Job, or with the paralysed woman referred to in Luke 13:16. But the purpose is to bring the offender to realize his sin and to turn him back in repentance to the Lord.

Of course, not all sickness is related to sin. Job was a righteous man who was tested by his physical sufferings but his 'comforters', who attributed this to his sin, were roundly rebuked by God. We must therefore not become simplistic in trying to trace physical or mental difficulties to specific sins. On the other hand, we do need to recognize that what we call stress-related diseases may often be sin-related. The stress is caused by envy, pride, bitterness or an unforgiving attitude, and these things may literally be killers. Sometimes, however, God allows sin to take its course, in order to bring us to our senses and to show us the need to put things right spiritually. We can recall the example of the prodigal son, who only came to his senses (Lk 15:17) when he met very adverse physical circumstances. Thus, in this case, it was more loving to cast the man off than to tolerate him and cause his eternal loss. So the action of church discipline is seen by the apostle as an action of love. Its object is not solely to punish, but to restore and heal. It is therapeutic. And, to judge from 2 Corinthians 2:5–11, that is exactly what happened, for it seems that the man did turn from his sin and in the second letter Paul has to encourage the church to receive him back as openly as Christ has received them.

But this would never have occurred had he not first been subject to discipline.

Paul's second principle in verses 6–8 is that sin needs dealing with. In these verses he delves deeper than the holding of a moral principle itself, to show the church why failure to grasp this nettle will be so disastrous for their future. To make the point, Paul used an everyday illustration from the kitchen. Only a small quantity of yeast will work its way through a much larger lump of dough. By the same analogy, we might say one rotten apple stored away can soon infect all the others. If sin is tolerated within one member, it may soon spread to others in the church. Indeed, they are already sinning as a church, by boasting about their spirituality, while actually tolerating gross evil in their midst. Already the evidence is there of the infection spreading. There is only one remedy and that has to be drastic—'Get rid of the old yeast' (verse 7a).

This Old Testament picture is an eloquent one. Before Passover, with its seven days of unleavened bread, every Jewish household would carefully search out all the stale yeast and leavened bread that might remain. Every bit had to be removed. This was a symbol of the clean break that Israel had to make with the corruption of the vices of Egypt at the time of the exodus. The unleavened bread of Passover was God's picture of the new life of holiness and separation to himself, for which he had redeemed them. They were 'a new batch without yeast'. That is the way God wants his people to live. But the Old Testament people had to be redeemed by the sacrifice of the Passover Lamb before they could be God's holy, new community. How much greater then, Paul argues, is *our* responsibility as Christians to put away sin, when we consider the identity of our Pascal Lamb. The Lord Jesus gave his life for us not just so that our past sin might be forgiven, but to make us new creations in Christ, 'as you really are' (verse 7).

Jesus has died to deal with the old sinful nature in us, to enable us to die daily, to be crucified with Christ, so that we no longer serve sin, but become purified holy people. We are therefore to keep the Festival by living the Christian life in sincerity and truth (verse 8). There is a responsibility incumbent upon every one of us as Christians to look upon our own consciences and wrestle with our own sins. As Gaston Deluz puts it, 'In the end, the only discipline that does not open the door to a new form of Pharisaism is the discipline each of us imposes on himself.' There are Christians who are professional heresy hunters and whose energy is largely devoted to tracking down the sins, imagined or real, of others. It is fatally easy for us to overlook the beam in our own eye while trying to pluck the speck from our brother's eye. But whenever sin attacks the church, it tests all the saints. So the emphasis within Scripture is upon looking to ourselves and making sure we do not become a means by which sin can infect the whole body. Far from being judgemental about our brothers and sisters, we are encouraged to look to ourselves. And if we are tempted towards any sort of spiritual pride, let us remember the warning that Paul gives later in this very letter: 'if you think you are standing firm, be careful that you don't fall!' (1 Cor 10:12).

Our problem is that we often fail to recognize such sin in our own lives. We may well say that we would not tolerate a gross moral evil of the sort with which the Corinthian church was prepared to live. But we do tolerate all sorts of sins which we defend as our own little weaknesses. I am thinking of the grudges and grievances that are allowed to persist for many years, the pride that will not admit when we are wrong, the bitterness and even hatred that can grow in our hearts towards others with whom we disagree. All the time we may seem to be doing so well as Christians outwardly, and we are so happy to let others believe it. But sin of this sort must also be dealt with in the church. It is the major hindrance to the spread of the gospel and that is why the greatest contribution we can make to evangelism in our own generation is our personal holiness. The more we deal with sin in our own lives, the more our personal witness and corporate life as the church of Christ will prove to be a magnet by which others are drawn to know him for themselves.

Jesus recognized that this would be an area of difficulty that his disciples would face in their corporate life.

> If your brother sins against you, go and show him his fault, just between the two of you. If he listens to you, you have won your brother over. But if he will not listen, take one or two others along, so that 'every matter may be established by the testimony of two or three witnesses.' If he refuses to listen to them, tell it to the church; and if he refuses to listen even to the church, treat him as you would a pagan or a tax collector. I tell you the truth, whatever you bind on earth will be bound in heaven, and whatever you loose on earth will be loosed in heaven. Again, I tell you that if two of you on earth agree about anything you ask for, it will be done for you by my Father in heaven. For where two or three come together in my name, there am I with them (Mt 18:15–20).

This is one of the very few gospel passages in which the Lord Jesus is teaching about the future church. He is making provision for difficulties to be resolved and sin to be dealt with. The sad fact is that so often we studiously ignore the process that he has given us. When a brother offends you, do you follow verse 15, or do you first go to someone else and pour it out to them? We have to work at this seriously. For example, when someone comes to complain about a fellow Christian we have to be determined to stop them and say, 'No, I'm sorry but we can't talk about that unless he's here.' What confidence and relaxedness would be promoted within a church if we all knew that talking about others behind their backs was out, because none of us would allow one another to do it. It would be difficult, but what joy it would bring! We would not be discussing the failure of others or mentioning them obliquely 'just for your prayers'. Rather we would be confronting one another with our weaknesses and failures, seeking, in the Spirit of Christ, to heal and restore.

But what if that response is not forthcoming? The Lord makes provision for further steps in verses 16 and 17. Churches have to be disciplined, but a forgiving spirit does not need such severe measures. Nevertheless, the Lord Jesus gives these provisions just because the whole business of love and forgiveness among his people matters so much. So if a brother refuses to listen, one or two others must go along with the one sinned against in order to establish the testimony. If he still further refuses, the group or the church as a whole is to become involved and the ultimate sanction is the removal of the brother from their fellowship.

Unforgiveness is one of the major causes of mental breakdown. It kills the spiritual life in those who cherish it and it affects their emotional, psychological and sometimes their physical health. Even more seriously, it kills the fellowship in which it is not dealt with. God means us to demonstrate his love by constant forgiveness in the church, for only that can adequately reflect the character and nature of the God who has so freely forgiven us. We are not to let the sun go down on our anger (Eph 4:26). We are to get rid of all bitterness (Eph 4:31). Therefore, we need to deal with any controversy, any unforgiving spirit which is present within our churches. The only way to do this effectively is by face-to-face meeting and by talking things through under the lordship of Christ, by seeking mutual forgiveness and a restoration of that which has been broken.

If this is a daunting prospect to us, then Matthew 18:19 is designed to be an encouragement to do it. So often we take the promises of verses 19 and 20 out of context. They do, of course, have a reference to all prayer that is made in the name and in the will of the Lord Jesus, but the primary reference is to praying that we shall be able truly to forgive and to have mercy. That prayer will always be answered because it is so dear to God's heart. Therefore, if I am finding it hard to forgive a brother, I need to ask one or two close friends to pray with me for grace to go God's way and to follow God's plan. Of course it is not easy. That is why the devil can use it as a frequent road-block to God's blessing really flowing through a local church. Peter thought he was doing well if he forgave his brother seven times. But Jesus sets before him what must have seemed the impossible target of forgiving seventy times seven, or so many times that you no longer count. If that is how God has forgiven us then we must be followers of our Lord. When General Ogilthorpe said to John Wesley, 'Sir, I never forgive,' he received the reply, 'Then I hope, sir, you never sin.' God's kingdom is one of free forgiveness and the church *must* demonstrate that in all her relationships. But that never means that the church is soft on sin within its members. Forgiveness is a totally different reality from tolerance.

As we return to 1 Corinthians 5, let us note that the chapter ends with a warning and a corrective:

> I have written you in my letter not to associate with sexually immoral people—not at all meaning the people of this world who are immoral, or the greedy and swindlers, or idolaters. In that case you would have to leave this world. But now I am writing you that you must not associate with anyone who calls himself a brother but is sexually immoral or greedy, an idolater or a slanderer, a drunkard or a swindler. With such a man do not even eat. What business is it of mine to judge those outside the church? Are you not to judge those inside? God will judge those outside. 'Expel the wicked man from among you' (1 Cor 5:9–13).

Paul reminds us that there is a wrong sort of Christian

separation which withdraws from the world almost totally. It is concerned to preserve its own apparent sanctity by having nothing to do with sinners. It withdraws into a Christian ghetto where the saints pride themselves on all the worldly things they do not do and fall for the sins of arrogance, jealousy, gossip and a judgemental spirit. These are all the Christian sins with which churches are turned in on themselves and which owe more to Pharisaism than to the Spirit of the Lord Jesus, who received sinners and ate with them. He prayed for his disciples, 'not that you [the Father] take them out of the world but that you protect them from the evil one' (Jn 17:15).

Any Christian who lives in this world of sin, as God intends, will inevitably rub shoulders with those described in 1 Corinthians 5:10. That is what the world is like. We are to be in it, to win it for Christ. We are not to become moral hermits. Nor is it our business to judge the world, as the Pharisees did. God alone is the judge and he will do right. Our responsibility is to set our own home in order, to look to others and guard the purity of the church, which is the thrust of verse 11. There is a right separation from one who calls himself a brother but who belies that by the sort of life he is living. Christianity is not compatible with the vices which verse 11 so graphically describes. To eat a meal was then, as it is now, a sign of friendship and fellowship. Paul says that the unfaithful brother must not be given that sign. There is to be a personal separation by each obedient believer from those whose flagrant sin brings discredit upon the name of the Lord Jesus. This is not on the grounds of their doctrinal confession in this case, which may still be perfectly orthodox, but on the grounds of their moral behaviour.

So as Christians we have a responsibility first to judge ourselves and then to judge our fellowship (verse 12b). We can safely leave the world in God's hands (verse 13a) but we have an obligation to act in church wherever it is necessary (verse 13b). Church discipline is thus the function of the whole people of God, to keep a constant watch on our character as the church of Jesus Christ. It is the special responsibility of leaders to provide the structures within which biblical discipline can be exercised. We are to give up pagan, worthless ways. But if we will not, then Satan's devices must be resisted. This will begin by persuasion and warning followed by rebuke and if necessary separation. Ultimately there may even be delivery into the hands of Satan. Church discipline is a serious matter and we do well to take it seriously. But over all this we must also remember that it has to be exercised in love or it is not an evidence of the life of Christ at all. Sadly, the history of the church is littered with examples of those whose attitudes have been anything but loving, and this is undoubtedly why so many are very reticent about this theme in the contemporary church. We must not allow ourselves to be deterred from the biblical task by the mistakes or excesses of the past. What we must do is to submit our lives and our churches to the authority of God's word and then to seek the fulness of God's Spirit so that we may exercise the truth with real love and compassion for one another. As we seek, by God's grace, to fulfil the pattern he has given us for the church, we can rely upon the Head to lead, to guide and to prosper our attempts to live more in accordance with his will.

10

When the Going Gets Tough

It is very clear both from the New Testament and from church history that the church of Jesus Christ cannot expect to fulfil the Lord's Great Commission without running into difficulties and opposition. Our own experience only confirms this truth. It has been so from the very start. The book we call the Acts of the Apostles is a record of the work of the Holy Spirit in a period of remarkable church growth and development, but alongside was fierce opposition. Furthermore, church history often shows that the church is at its strongest and spreading most rapidly when the opposition is at its most intense. But whether or not fierce antagonists and antagonism is the experience of any of us at this particular moment, we are certainly to understand from the Bible that tests, trials and problems are the norm for God's people as we live in a hostile and fallen world.

If that surprises and if we find it strange that we should face difficulties and trials, we are really being very naïve as Christians. The going will get tough. The Bible clearly teaches us to expect that. But when that happens, then the tough get going! Of course, that can mean two things. It can be a cynical comment on those who are prepared to

147

fight until they face the enemy but who run when the enemy is identified. The 'tough' get going in the sense that they put as much distance between them and the conflict as they possibly can. That attitude is enshrined in our characteristically English proverb, 'Discretion is the better part of valour.' But the tough getting going can mean something very different, namely that opposition only serves to strengthen the nerve and determination to fight on, and to triumph. When the going gets tough, then the tough roll up their sleeves and accept the challenge. The church in history has done and still does both of those things. There have been times when all of us as Christians have run from the battle, when we have failed to face up to the challenges. But there have also been other glorious times when, in the midst of the toughest situations, Christians have called upon the power and grace of God, and found that he has enabled them to fight and win. That has been proved to be true, and I am sure in our lives as well.

In 2 Timothy 3:12 Paul says that, 'Everyone who wants to live a godly life in Christ Jesus will be persecuted.' All Christians worthy of the name are, according to the Bible, listed in the Lord's army. If we are part of that army, therefore, we are neither to be surprised nor aggrieved if and when we get hurt. War has that effect, and our task now is to look at how we are to learn, from the experience of the early church, to cope when the going gets tough.

Such testing experiences can come to the church in a variety of situations. In the next two chapters we shall be concerning ourselves with internal challenges and difficulties which clamoured to be dealt with before they blew the young congregations apart. Disagreements over the administrative and practical difficulties (Acts 6) can be as potentially damaging to the church as head-on persecution. Similarly, the challenge of integrating and harmonizing within the church converts from very different cultural backgrounds (Acts 15), the challenge of heterogeneity, was an issue of vital importance if the Gentile church was to take root and grow. One cannot help feeling that one of the devil's most frequent and successful methods for side-tracking the church is to divert an over-large portion of our time, energy and manpower to dealing with internal problems; putting out brush-fires, smoothing ruffled fur, instead of fulfilling the great commandments Christ has left us.

But in this chapter, we shall study how they dealt with opposition that came from outside. The scene is set in Acts chapter 3. Peter and John had just healed a lame man. He had been sitting at the Beautiful Gate of the temple for many years, asking those going into worship to give him alms. It is probable that every devout Jew in Jerusalem knew this man. Certainly regular visitors to the temple would be very familiar with him. Then, in the name of Jesus of Nazareth, Peter and John commanded him to rise up and walk, which he did, 'walking and jumping, and praising God' (Acts 3:1–10). This not only provided Peter with a great preaching opportunity, but it also aroused the opposition of the Jewish authorities, who arrested both Peter and John, keeping them in jail overnight. But while the messengers of Christ were in prison, the word of the Lord was active; 'Many who heard the message believed and the number of men grew to about five thousand' (Acts 4:4). So here we have a picture of the messengers shut up in jail, but the word they preached still active, alive and powerful, changing people's lives.

The next day Peter and John were brought before the Sanhedrin to explain their action. They were asked, 'By what power or by what name did you do this?' (verse 7). This is the first record in the Bible of any official contact between the religious authorities and the infant church. The authorities' response was hostile, which provokes an important question: what is it about the Christian faith that generates such opposition? Look at verse 9, where Peter says, 'If we are being called to account today for an act of kindness shown to a cripple and are asked how he was healed, then know this, you and everyone else in Israel: It is by the name of Jesus Christ . . . that this man stands before you completely healed.'

Surely, one would think, everybody would want to rejoice in this. Here was an act of kindness done to a crippled man, who was now standing completely well and whole. Isn't that the very substance of Christianity? Then why should it provoke such opposition? The answer is that if you think that that is the substance of the Christian faith, you are right and wrong at the same time. Many people are very happy with a Christianity that consists simply of acts of kindness, but that is only one ingredient of the Christian faith.

Look at verse 10 again: 'It is by the name of Jesus Christ of Nazareth, whom you crucified but whom God raised from the dead, that this man stands before you completely healed.' That is the crux of the matter. They were arrested, not because of the miracle, but because of the preaching. Go back to verse 2: 'The apostles were teaching the people and proclaiming in Jesus the resurrection of the dead.' That is why they were arrested. The Sadducees did not believe in the resurrection in any sense so that to have this doctrine proclaimed in the temple and connected with the hated name of Jesus of Nazareth, whom they had only recently removed, was more than they could tolerate. Thus, the opposition was directed against the person of Jesus, against the claim being made by the apostles that he was the Christ and the Son of God. That is why they ended up in jail. They began to suffer for the sake of the name of the Lord Jesus Christ.

Christians sometimes suffer today because we are unwise, or because we are even offensive in the way in which we conduct ourselves or our witness. If we suffer for those reasons, then that is not persecution and we must not justify our insensitivity by honouring the consequences of our actions with that title. But where there is direct opposition, because of clear testimony to the person of Jesus, do not be surprised if you suffer. Do not imagine either that it is directed against you personally. It is aimed against him. But if we bear his mind—that is our privilege—we must expect to suffer as he did. Many of you reading this may well have experienced this sort of suffering over the last few months. In a period of six months or so in my own church, we experienced all sorts of attacks on members of our church family—physical suffering, emotional suffering, difficulties in personal relationships, intractable problems about the future, perplexities, direct opposition and so on. It is no coincidence that this was also a time of considerable evangelistic effectiveness and church growth.

We are to see these attacks as part of our suffering for the name of the Lord Jesus. It is no accident that these things happen. If a church takes seriously the Great Commission and goes out in obedience to Christ to make him known, if it proclaims the name of Jesus within its society by the way it lives and by what it says, it must expect to meet opposition. The situation will get tough. Satan is not going to bother to attack a church that is asleep, rather one that is awake and reaching out. So we must look closely here and try to learn from the Scriptures how these early Christians dealt with the challenges because, like them, we too are on the victory side.

Jesus has authority and resources that are more than sufficient for us to be able to cope with the opposition. And if we can learn from this chapter how he pulled them through victoriously, and went on adding to the church those who were being saved, then we can find strength, encouragement and resources for ourselves, so that when the going gets tough, we too are enabled to persevere.

Let us examine three strands which are the key to understanding the early church's ability to keep going. The first is in verses 10–12. Peter said,

> It is by the name of Jesus Christ of Nazareth whom you crucified but whom God raised from the dead, that this man stands before you completely healed. He is 'the stone you builders rejected, which has become the capstone.' Salvation is found in no-one else, for there is no other name under heaven given to men by which we must be saved (Acts 4:10b–12).

These verses highlight the clarity of their witness. Far from being intimidated by the opposition, the apostles refused to compromise their message one jot. Right at the heart of their opponents' citadel, Peter proclaimed the power of the name of the living Christ. Such boldness is clearly and specifically related to the ministry of the Holy Spirit. Verse 8 states very definitely that before Peter spoke he was filled with the Spirit. Similarly, verse 31 affirms that they were all filled with the Holy Spirit and spoke the word of God boldly. The one was the cause of the other. So their clear witness was dependent on their being filled with the Spirit. Indeed this is what Jesus said in Acts 1:8. He promised that the disciples would receive the Holy Spirit and as his power came upon them they would be enabled to become his witnesses in Jerusalem, Judea, Samaria and unto the uttermost parts of the earth. We must understand that we cannot be witnesses to Jesus without the Holy Spirit. It is the Spirit's great work to take the things of Christ and make them real and precious. He loves to exalt the Lord Jesus. The great purpose of the coming of the Spirit, in the New Testament, is to give Christians power to witness to Christ. None of the ways in which the early church met the fierce opposition ranged against them was independent of God.

The ability to cope did not then lie in Peter and John,

but lay in the Lord. Peter and John were not supermen. It was only a few weeks earlier that they had all run away when Jesus was arrested. When Peter was challenged by a serving maid regarding his loyalty to Jesus he had denied him with oaths and curses. But now, when he is asked the same question by the religious authorities, he begins to accuse them of murdering the Son of God and declares that there is no other name in which there is salvation. What has happened to this man? He has been filled with the Spirit. Pentecost is what has happened. The Holy Spirit has come and taken up residence in his personality and the fulness of the Spirit enables Peter to witness, with clarity and courage.

We must remember also that it was not a once-for-all experience, but something that was repeated and so became an ongoing reality for them, as indeed it should also be for us. When you become a Christian you receive the Holy Spirit who is a person, indivisible. You cannot receive half the Spirit or 63% of the Spirit, any more than you have a percentage of a guest to stay with you for the weekend. Either the whole guest comes to you, or none of him! In the same way, as a believer, you receive the *whole* Spirit. The Spirit comes into your life in order to fill you with the limitless resources of the life of God. If you will allow him to fill every part of your life, as you yield to him, he will take you and use you as a witness. But you need constantly to be renewed in the Spirit. That is why Paul's exhortation to the Ephesians reads, literally, 'be continually being filled with the Spirit.' Or, to paraphrase the New English Bible, 'Let the Holy Spirit keep on filling you' (Eph 5:18). So here, in Acts 4:31, being filled with the Spirit is the biblical description of what the disciples experienced. They had just been filled on the day of Pentecost in Acts chapter 2. Peter was again filled in Acts 4:8. Here they were filled once more. For it is not that there is some special second blessing that you have to somehow acquire and thereafter you possess the fulness of the Spirit. It is that every day of your life is to be open to the limitless resources of the Holy Spirit, who flows through all those who are open to him, to make them witnesses to Jesus.

Only God himself can provide these resources, but it is his delight to equip his people, so that we may confidently affirm that there is a constant source of fresh supply, for our every new experience of human need. When we witness, we are sometimes tempted to water down or compromise the message. Only the Lord can keep us true. But look at how he did so here. He enabled Peter and John to proclaim uncompromisingly the person of Jesus. We can only witness with reality as we rely on the same Holy Spirit, as we say to God, 'Lord, I can't do this, but you can. Please accomplish your purposes through me.' For if we see our Christian living in that light we shall not be afraid to witness, nor shall we regard evangelism as something that we try to turn on at any given moment. It will be the natural overflow of the life that is within us.

So the apostles faced opposition by reminding themselves who Jesus really is and then proclaiming this to others. They focused on the person of Jesus. It is 'by the name of Jesus Christ of Nazareth' (verse 10). That is his title. He is Christ, the Son of God, the eternally divine One. He is Jesus who is the Christ, who was crucified, but who has been raised from the dead. They proved his resurrection because they had witnessed it. We today are the recipients of their witness and they say he is still active in healing and in giving life. It is by him that this man was healed.

But the natural progression from the proclamation of Christ as the Son of God is seen in their declaration of his lordship in verse 11: 'The stone you builders rejected . . . has become the capstone.' That is a quotation from Psalm 118:22 which refers in the first place to the king as the

leader of the nation, but then to the Messiah as the
sovereign Lord, so that it is, in effect, a claim to sovereignty. Only a few weeks earlier, Jesus had applied those very
same words from that Psalm to the religious leaders so
pointedly that Matthew tells us that they knew he was
talking about them as the ungodly builders who rejected
God's foundation stone (Mt 21:45). Here Peter and the
others declare that this Christ, the Son of God, was Jesus
of Nazareth. He is alive; he is Lord; God has made him the
foundation stone. And then in verse 12 they also proclaimed him as the only way of salvation. Jesus alone had
saved this lame man and God has exalted this Jesus to a
position of authority, which cannot be shared with
anybody. So if God has declared him to be Saviour, he is
without parallel. There is no other name in which salvation is to be found.

These were precisely the ingredients that intensified the
opposition then, as they still do today. But the apostles did
not give up despite that. They kept pointing to Christ.

Secondly, the apostles faced the opposition by courageous obedience.

> Then they [the Sanhedrin] called them in again and
> commanded them not to speak or teach at all in the name of
> Jesus. But Peter and John replied, 'Judge for yourselves
> whether it is right in God's sight to obey you rather than
> God. For we cannot help speaking about what we have seen
> and heard' (Acts 4:18–20).

We are told that the Sanhedrin authorities were amazed
because the apostles had no formal theological training
(verse 13). The term used, 'unschooled, ordinary men', is
a technical term, meaning simply that they had not been to
the rabbis' schools. They had not been to theological
college; but they had been with Jesus. And no one could
deny the miracle that had happened. There was the man
healed, in front of them. It was always a problem for

Christ's opponents—and indeed it still is—because the change that Jesus makes in people's lives is undeniable. They had to attribute these miracles either to magic or to occult forces, which is what they did in the first century. You can find various attacks on Christianity, saying that it uses magic, occult powers, but it was of course none of these things.

Nevertheless, the Sanhedrin were determined that this new movement should spread no further, so they ordered the apostles to speak no longer in Jesus' name. The opposition has become much tougher. They are not just questioning now but giving them a command: no more gospel preaching (verse 18). Christians have often faced that sort of challenge down the centuries and some still do today. The apostles met it with a courageous application of two principles that Jesus had taught them, and to which they saw themselves as being obedient. These principles are embodied in these words of Jesus: 'Render therefore unto Caesar the things which are Caesar's; and unto God the things that are God's' (Mt 22:21 AV). On the first part, they did not defy their rulers, in the sense of despising their authority. They did not say that they were not going to listen to them at all and storm out of the building. They refused to obey them but they did so only because their allegiance to God came first. The higher authority must be obeyed (verse 19). 'For we cannot help speaking about what we have seen and heard' (verse 20). We are called to be Christ's witnesses and we must obey that higher authority.

We have to be very careful in our application of this. Let me put to you firstly a false application of this principle. Here is someone trying to be a witness for Christ at work. He spends so much time on evangelizing other people that his employer rightly becomes very irate about it and says, 'You're stealing the time you should be giving to me, in order to spread your religion to others.' The Christian replies, 'Render to Caesar what is Caesar's, and to God what is God's.' He imagines that he can go on with his practice simply because of the justification that God has called him to be a witness.

Now he would be wrong because he is not rendering to Caesar what is his right. Caesar in the form of his employer is paying him money to work and he is therefore obligated to give the maximum amount of energy and concentration to that work. If he fails to do that, he is not rendering to Caesar what is Caesar's due. That is a fundamental principle. By contrast, when Caesar tries to overrule a Christian's obedience to a plain divine command, for example when the state says no more gospel preaching, then there is only one course of action open to the Christian, because obedience to God comes before the commands of men, before any religious or political system.

And Peter reminds the Sanhedrin in verse 19 that they do not speak with God's voice. He contrasts obeying the authorities and obeying God. The Sanhedrin thought they were speaking with the voice of God, but Peter refutes this. If they really were God's mouthpiece, he argues, they would hardly stop Christians speaking in the name of Jesus. So there was here a courageous act of obedience that put God's priorities first in their lives.

Only a person who lives under God's sovereignty every day, whose life is characterized by detailed daily obedience, will have the courage to assert that principle when the going gets tough. If our lives are marked by a succession of little compromises, as far as being a Christian is concerned, when the going gets tough we shall collapse. But if we live every day in obedience to Christ, as far as we are able, relying on his Spirit, then when the tough time comes there will be a strength present, a habit of mind and a direction of life, that will enable us to say, though our knees may knock, 'I must obey God rather than man.'

Thirdly, the apostles met the threat of concerted opposition with corporate prayer.

On their release, Peter and John went back to their own people and reported all that the chief priests and elders had said to them. When they heard this, they raised their voices together in prayer to God. 'Sovereign Lord,' they said, 'you made the heaven and the earth and the sea, and everything in them. You spoke by the Holy Spirit through the mouth of your servant, our father David: "Why do the nations rage and peoples plot in vain? The kings of the earth take their stand and the rulers gather together against the Lord and against his Anointed One." Indeed Herod and Pontius Pilate met together with the Gentiles and the people of Israel in this city to conspire against your holy servant, Jesus, whom you anointed. They did what your power and will had decided beforehand should happen. Now, Lord, consider their threats and enable your servants to speak your word with great boldness. Stretch out your hand to heal and perform miraculous signs and wonders through the name of your holy servant, Jesus' (Acts 4:23–30).

I like verse 23 because it shows what the natural gravitational pull was for the apostles. They went back to the fellowship—their own people—and reported what had happened. Together they then came to God in prayer. They were not standing alone. They were called upon to be obedient, but they had this great privilege of taking all that they were facing back to their brothers and sisters and in raising their voices in prayer together to God. Here is a great resource when the going gets tough—praying together. We need one another to stimulate and encourage our prayers. That is why I am so excited about increasing the prayer ingredient in house groups today, because once we begin to share openly about our struggles, prayer is the natural response. It is such a strength and encouragement to be able to share with others. If a group of Christians who are studying the word of God cannot pray together, there is something seriously lacking in their study. If a group of Christians do not find it natural to undergird their fellowship meetings with prayer, there is something fundamentally distorted in their concept of fellowship. If we are concerned for one another in any meaningful sense, we should naturally want to pray together. We do not have to be embarrassed; we belong to the same family.

And here we have only to look at the ingredients of this marvellous pattern of prayer to see how God uses this means of his grace in order to strengthen and increase their resolve. Firstly in the pattern there was unity in their praying. They raised their voices together. The older versions say, 'With one accord to God.' They realized that they were all in the battle together. There was no sense of leaving Peter and John to get on with it or imagining that because they were apostles the rest of the body could ignore their predicament. That would be sub-Christian thinking and a denial of true fellowship. When we bind together, special power is available.

Secondly, they called on the God of power: 'Sovereign Lord,' they said, 'you made the heaven and the earth and the sea, and everything in them' (verse 24). What a vision of God they had! Their prayer was no desperate cry to a weak, disinterested deity, who could perhaps be persuaded to work some help for them. But how much of our prayer is like that? They realized the God they were coming to. This was the God without whom nothing exists, who has the whole world in his hands and who had allowed none of these things to happen apart from his sovereign will. So they rest themselves on God's government of the whole world and on his power to achieve everything that he wills. They call on him as sovereign Lord, our Lord. How often do we pray like that? Is it too often, 'Dear Lord, perhaps you could find it in your heart to help a little here and squeeze a little blessing there'?

When the going gets tough, you need a great God, a

God of power, majesty and sovereignty.

How did they know he was a sovereign Lord? Because they relied on the truths of Scripture (verses 25–28), the third ingredient in this pattern of prayer. In their praying, they quoted Psalm 2:1–2. They allowed what God had already said to them in that Psalm to shape what they said to him in their praying. That is the great secret of effective prayer, to rely on Scripture, to read Scripture, to take the promises of Scripture and build on them in our prayers. What had happened to the Lord Jesus was in fulfilment of God's word (verse 27). We can see their view of life. That is where Scripture takes you. There are no accidents, because God is in control. And as that shapes your mind, it will shape your prayers—'And this battle we are going through now, Lord, this toughness you have called us to face; that too is part of your sovereign will. Your power is involved with us in it. All the plotting of your enemies is included under your sovereignty. It is only permitted by your will and you are going to frustrate those plots and defeat them. That is part of your sovereign will too.' We are to build on Scripture in our prayers.

All true theology leads us to pray. If it does not bring you to your knees it has not yet permeated your being. All true understanding of God leads us to pray. 'Sovereign Lord, you are in control. Work your will in us.'

As the fourth ingredient, they asked for specifics (verses 29 and 30). They dealt with their fears in the immediate situation by prayer and by petition. They took their threatenings to God and said, 'Lord, consider them.' That means, 'Lord, you deal with them. You are the true Court of Appeal and we are giving these threatenings to you. And for ourselves? Lord, we want to pray for ourselves not that you would give us permission to be silent in the face of the gathering storm, not that you would send others instead of us to do this job, but that you would enable your bond slaves to speak your word with great boldness.' They had already identified as the Lord's servants. They had no will of their own. They knew they were committed to be witnesses, so what did they ask for? Grace to do the difficult thing, and to do it effectively.

In response to that special need, God gave them a special answer: 'they were all filled with the Holy Spirit and spoke the word of God boldly' (verse 31). God answers specific prayers. But notice that they wanted above everything else Christ's glory, so they asked for miraculous signs and wonders to be done through the name of the Lord Jesus. They wanted these mighty works to be demonstrated in order that Jesus might be glorified. That was their greatest concern and desire; not their safety, nor their satisfaction, but the glory of Jesus. That was what they now lived for—the letting loose of God's power so that Jesus' name might be proclaimed everywhere.

That is always the most effective counter-argument to all the threatening of Satan, for the glory of Jesus to be revealed. That is what they prayed for and that is the sort of praying that produces results. The place was shaken. As they had appealed to the God of sovereignty, in response he assured them of his power and authority by showing it first in the physical realm, shaking the house, and then in a new bestowal of spiritual energy upon them which proved beyond all doubt that their sovereign God was indeed answering their prayers. For when God answers, he does not just send his blessings, he brings them. He does not despatch us a packet marked 'perseverance' or 'power'. He comes to us personally to *be* our perseverance and our power, by filling us freshly with his Spirit, to give us courage and new vision; above all to give us the ability to be obedient, because the ultimate answer to all our needs is in God himself. So it was with God here, that after they had prayed the whole company of disciples was filled with God again. There is always fresh grace to meet fresh need. And the Holy Spirit met their specific need.

Specific prayer requests bring specific answers. It is all summed up in verse 33: 'With great power the apostles continued to testify to the resurrection of the Lord Jesus, and much grace was with them all.' I have underlined in my Bible the two phrases 'great power' and 'much grace'. When God's people pray, the Holy Spirit grants that sort of answer. He is the power which strengthens us. He toughens us, so that we can keep going, enabling us to be more than conquerors through him who loved us. His is the grace that sweetens us and refines us, to make us loving and able to do the will of God, in the way of God. How else can you cope with life, when the going gets tough? What else do you need to cope with life than 'great power' and 'much grace'? We have our Bibles and we have our knees; we have just to use them both!

11

Challenges That Test Priorities

Whenever progress occurs in the church it is unsettling. People begin to feel quite uncomfortable and complaint is never far away. I rather like the story of the centenarian who was being interviewed on his birthday.

'You must have seen lots of changes,' enthused the young reporter.

'Yes, I have,' the old man replied, 'and I'm proud to say I've been against them all!'

But what surfaces as complaint is sometimes a vote of confidence in things as they are and so it should not be ignored. On the other hand, it can be an expression of problems that have been overlooked, of difficulties just buried beneath the surface, which need to be attended to quickly, if further progress is not to be impeded. Such challenges can be a blessing in disguise if they lead us to clarify and reaffirm our priorities. That is what we find happening to the young church in Acts chapter 6.

In those days when the number of disciples was increasing, the Grecian Jews among them complained against those of the Aramaic-speaking community because their widows were being overlooked in the daily distribution of food. So the Twelve gathered all the disciples together and said, 'It would not be right for us to neglect the ministry of the word of God in order to wait on tables. Brothers, choose seven men from among you who are known to be full of the Spirit and wisdom. We will turn this responsibility over to them and will give our attention to prayer and the ministry of the word.' This proposal pleased the whole group. They chose Stephen, a man full of faith and of the Holy Spirit; also Philip, Procorus, Nicanor, Timon, Parmenas and Nicolas from Antioch, a convert to Judaism. They presented these men to the apostles, who prayed and laid their hands on them. So the word of God spread. The number of disciples in Jerusalem increased rapidly, and a large number of priests became obedient to the faith' (Acts 6:1–7).

In the previous chapter we saw how the early church reacted when the going got tough, in coping with the challenge of external opposition. Acts 5 reminds us that this was not something that went away. In fact the opposition increased as time went by. Peter and John were hauled before the authorities and Peter and the other apostles give an account of their activity. The result is that the Sanhedrin called the apostles in and had them flogged (Acts 5:40). Then they ordered them not to speak in the name of Jesus and let them go. But as the opposition increased and with it their physical suffering, so did the apostles' determination to fulfil the Master's Commission.

The apostles left the Sanhedrin, rejoicing because they had been counted worthy of suffering disgrace for the Name. Day after day, in the temple courts and from house to house, they never stopped teaching and proclaiming the good news that Jesus is the Christ (verses 41–42).

It is against this background that Luke directs our attention to a very different challenge in chapter 6. This time the challenge comes from within the church: in those days as the word of God was spreading and the number of disciples was increasing there arose (literally) a murmuring among the disciples.

That word 'murmuring' is an interesting one. It does not come through very clearly in the New International Version because the translators have rendered it, 'The Grecian Jews . . . complained.' But the word is translated elsewhere in the New Testament as 'whispering', or 'complaining' or 'grumbling'. Put the three together and you have a very clear picture of what was happening. The gospel is spreading, the apostles are suffering but they have tremendous power through the Spirit to teach and proclaim the good news. But what happens among the people of God? There is a whispering, complaining and grumbling. I want to call it 'chuntering'. Chuntering is as old as the history of the church and it is potentially lethal.

This tendency is a killer, make no mistake about it. It is one of Satan's most powerful weapons in destroying churches. These things are written for our learning, so we can ask three questions of the verses in front of us.

Firstly, what was the problem? Verse 1 makes it very clear. The Grecian Jews complained against those of the Aramaic-speaking community because their widows were being overlooked in the daily distribution of food. To understand this better we need to uncover some of the background. The Jerusalem church was largely composed of Jews, but the Jewish nation—and the church was no exception—was divided into two main groupings. There were the Hellenists (or Grecian Jews) who spoke Greek as their first language and there were the Hebrews, who spoke Aramaic, the native language of Palestine. These two groups were very different.

The Greek-speaking Jews, the Hellenists, owed their separate identity to the dispersion of the Jews throughout the Gentile world. They came under the influence of Greek culture and spoke the Greek language naturally. They had grown up in a Greek context. The Old Testament that they used was the Septuagint, the Greek translation, and, of course, when they became Christians they brought their culture and their special characteristics into the church.

But the Hebrews, the Aramaic speakers, were born and bred in Israel, a fact of which they were very proud. They were inhabitants of the land that God had given. They did not speak Greek, but Aramaic. They did not use the Septuagint, but the original Hebrew scriptures. They despised Gentile culture and clung tenaciously to their traditional Jewish ways, so that the rabbis in Palestine taught, 'Cursed is he who teaches his son the learning of the Greeks.' (You might be tempted to agree if you have ever had to study it at school!) Further, the Hebrew Christians were very conservative in their culture and customs.

These two bodies of very different cultural backgrounds were now brought together, by the gospel, into one family—the church in Jerusalem. Did they all automatically get on with each other? Of course not. There were deep, strongly held differences, just the kind of situation which Satan always likes to exploit. There was an apparently genuine grievance here. The Hellenistic widows were being overlooked. That was not really surprising because they were probably quite numerous. Many of the Jews of the dispersion who lived outside Israel longed to end their days in Jerusalem. Consequently there were always many widows in the city of Jerusalem who, after their husbands had died somewhere in Greece or Cyprus or Syria, came to Jerusalem. And as the number of believers multiplied, so too would the number of Greek-speaking widows. Therefore, the task of meeting their needs, because they were immigrants without family homes and often without very much financial support, would become very great and the Hellenistic widows were especially vulnerable to being overlooked. They failed to receive their fair share. You can imagine what happened. 'Why should the Aramaic-speaking community all be well-catered for and our Hellenistic widows be forgotten? After all, the apostles are Aramaic speakers, aren't they? You see the church leaders are on *their* side really.' It was a problem that was genuine. At root it was a problem of growth but there was much more to it than that. We need to dig deeper and see that the problem actually unfolds several challenges which the young church was facing.

There were three challenges in all, each of which can surface as the result of problems in any community of believers. The first challenge was to unity. This comes from the way in which the whole issue surfaced, in the form of a chuntering. Verse 1 shows us that the Grecian Jews tackled the problem in the wrong way, although theirs was a genuine grievance. So, how should they have tackled it? The right way was for those who felt that they were not being treated properly to go to the leadership in a clear and loving manner and point out the problem. That is what they failed to do and that is what Christians hardly ever do. Instead they chunter. And they began to personalize the identity of the problem as 'them': 'It's their fault.' That is one of the devil's most powerful tactical weapons. If he can get Christians in a church to stop talking about 'us' and to divide into 'us' and 'them', then he has scored a major breakthrough. And he will do it on whatever grounds he can find, even on what colour the hymnbooks are, if he cannot find any other grounds. He will find some ground to divide 'us' from 'them' and so split the church into factions and camps. That is why the scripture says, 'watch out for those who cause divisions and put obstacles in your way . . . Keep away from them' (Rom 16:17). This was a threat to unity because once this sort of chuntering gains a hold the church is already beginning to crumble. We must be warned about this, especially if God has given us in our own local church a considerable measure of unity. This is his gift, which we should treasure and be eager to preserve. So I must emphasize that the sin of murmuring is a very serious one. It threatens the life of the church because it denies and attacks the unity that God has brought about through the gospel. When we have grievances, we must be open with one another, we must share them face to face and not talk about them behind other people's backs. They must be brought forward lovingly and carefully discussed with the leadership of the fellowship, so that we can understand and solve them together.

I am not saying that we should all agree together on everything. That would be absolutely impossible. But Christians are not to react in a situation of grievance by murmuring. It was murmuring that kept Israel out of the promised land and it is murmuring that still destroys churches. Let us not pretend it does not happen. It is happening far too frequently in many congregations. If the sin of murmuring begins to break down fellowship, God regards that as very serious indeed. 'Don't you know that you yourselves are God's temple and that God's Spirit lives in you? If anyone destroys God's temple God will destroy him; for God's temple is sacred, and you are that temple' (1 Cor 3:16, 17).

The 'you' there is plural. Paul is talking about the church. He says that if anyone either destroys or tries to destroy the church of God, that is a very grave sin indeed. So what the early Christians faced was a serious threat, in that by going the wrong way about things and sowing seeds of complaint, whispering and grumbling, they were in danger of breaking up the very church that God was building.

Secondly, there was a challenge to progress. In Acts 6:2 the apostles articulate the crucial question: how were they going to spend their time? Here was the challenge that they had to face. There in verse 2 is a far reaching choice between two types of ministry. With the growth of the church, the apostles could not possibly perform both. There was the ministry of the word of God and that of tables, as they called it. Unfortunately, our English translation obscures this, but the word translated at the end of verse 1 as 'distribution' is the same word that is translated 'ministry' in verse 2 and is used again in verse 4 as the ministry of the word. It is the word *diakonia*, which of course gives us our word deacon. The verbal form has as its root meaning 'to wait at table' which is the way it is used in verse 2. The apostles realized that if they were to get caught up with the details of the daily food distribution to the needy, they would have to neglect some other aspect of the ministry. They were realistic enough to see that it would be their prayer and teaching ministries that would suffer. To put it in our terms, if they were to cope with the pastoral advance of the growing church, then they would have to neglect the ministries of prayer, evangelism and teaching. They could not go on adding to their responsibilities indefinitely, so they present the alternatives very clearly to the disciples. This is the challenge that would test their priorities. What is the church going to do? The apostles had no doubt at all about what was right in this situation. They said very clearly that it would not be right for them to neglect the ministry of the word of God in order to wait on tables (verse 2). The implication is clearly that it would not be pleasing to God. That was not their calling.

I wonder if you would agree with that. In fact the church was not asked to agree—they were told. The reason is surely that if the apostles had been neglecting the ministry of the word of God, in evangelism and in upbuilding the new Christians, in order to deal with the material needs of the widows, then the church would have been guilty of using its leadership to minister to itself. The church might have been comfortable and it might have grown fat, but it would not have grown strong. In effect it would have become a sort of Jewish synagogue. Instead of being the only human society that exists for those who are not yet its members, it would have focused everything on its own membership.

The apostles affirmed that this was not the way to go forward because it was not God's plan. It is the priority of evangelism and of up-building the people of God to which the church is called. Whatever we have to sacrifice in order to deal with that, we must make that sacrifice gladly, which is what the apostles are doing here. They had been given a priority by God (as you see in verse 4): 'We . . . will give our attention to prayer and the ministry of the word.' And because they stuck to that priority, because they did not allow themselves to be deflected into being administrators, the gospel spread and the church developed into a missionary church, with a worldwide vision. But, humanly speaking, it could so easily have gone the other way. On this little hinge, the great door swung. So it was a challenge to progress, because if they made the wrong decision, the church would have become inward-looking and it would never have reached out as God wanted it to.

Thirdly, there was a challenge to leadership. The way that the apostles dealt with this challenge is very instructive. Notice in verse 2 that they brought it out in the open. They did not deal with it behind closed doors but gathered all the disciples together and explained to them what was happening. Public discussion and accountability, if used like this, within a church are very important. There is no hole-in-a-corner attitude here. All is done in the open, with no manipulating behind the scenes. The whole church is affected, so the whole church must be involved. But notice too that the leaders did not come to the church and ask the church what they should do. They came to the church and said, 'It wouldn't be right for us to do this. We're going to do that.' Did they act in that way because they were dictators? I don't think so. But certainly the church is not a democracy. The apostles proposed a solution that the people accepted (verse 5) because it was one in which they were involved: 'This proposal pleased the whole group.' There is no dichotomy between the leadership and the people, or between the clergy and the laity, as we might put it today. That did not exist. But those who are given leadership by God—and there must always be God-ordained leaders in any church community—recognized their responsibility to involve the community in making a decision. They came, however, with a clear and strongly-held recommendation.

Christian leadership is a co-operative effort. The apostles were not dictators, but they did have authority, and if any church is to function, the responsibility of leadership also carries with it authority. People who are elected or appointed to do a job must be allowed to do it. So the leadership in Jerusalem fulfilled its role in identifying God's priority and instructing the people on how the situation should be met, and the congregation received the word and put it into effect. It was part of the apostles' leadership to direct the church to the sort of men who ought to do this task.

So they said in verse 3, 'Brothers, choose seven men from among you who are known to be full of the Spirit and wisdom' and the church responds. They chose Stephen and the other six listed there in verse 5 to do that job. As the church expands, it is constantly in need of Christians who are full of wisdom and faith, because they are full of the Holy Spirit. Look down to verse 8. It speaks there of Stephen as 'a man full of God's grace and power'. That is the kind of person who is needed in churches, people who are full of God's grace and power. They are the qualities we need to look for to be able to move ahead as a church. God give us more men and women like that! God give us a heart to be men and women like that, full of grace and power. The two go together. Grace speaks of the character of the Lord Jesus. Power speaks of the dynamic of the Spirit in our lives. We need both if the job is going to be done, a church of men and women full of the Spirit and wisdom.

So they met the challenge and in the right way. It was not a misfortune that the challenge came or that the issue was raised. It was perfectly right that they faced it, otherwise the church might have disintegrated. We all face challenges and we shall go on facing them as long as we are the people of God on earth. But the way we deal with them is the crucial thing. They can challenge both our unity and our progress. We need to meet them with a recognition of God's will as revealed in Scripture, with a respect for the authority of Scripture as mediated through those who lead the church. If and where they are wrong they need to be corrected because we are all under the authority of Scripture and of the Spirit. But there must be leadership. Nowhere in the New Testament do you find the idea that the church is a democracy and that in any situation we ought to sit down and wait and see which view can secure 51% in order to determine which way to go forward. In my own church, a few years ago, we faced the problem of meeting an overcrowding problem in the mornings, either by increasing the television relay system or by holding two morning services. At the first survey, the congregation was almost equally divided in their preference between the two. It took us a year of congregational forum meetings, in which all the difficulties and problems were aired and discussed, of special prayer meetings and many leadership discussions, before we were able to move forward. But when we took the decision to move to two services, 98% of the church declared themselves in favour. Challenges like this may well be God's way of binding us more closely together.

Lastly, what was the outcome? We find the wonderful result in verse 7: 'So the word of God spread. The number of disciples . . . increased rapidly.' The outcome was progress and development. I rejoice to see, as I study God's dealings with his people in Scripture, that all our crises are potential growth points. It is true both in our own lives and in that of the church. What makes them worth while is that situations like this can actually be points at which you grow in fellowship and in love for one another. The trials and pressures we are so often under are the means the Lord uses to assure us of his love, to show us his grace and to speed us on in the task he has given us.

The church met this challenge by delegation. At one and the same time this increased the ministry team and narrowed the responsibilities of each participant. The apostles conveyed their advice to the whole church, who in turn made the selection. Seven men were chosen, not because they were good administrators, not because they were popular people, but because they were godly. They were men full of the Spirit and wisdom. Moreover, they were representative of the Greeks, because all the names of the men who were chosen had Greek names. It was surely gracious of the Hebrews to pick out seven Greeks to help their fellow Greeks. They were set apart to meet a particular need (verse 3): 'choose seven men from among you who are known to be full of the Spirit and wisdom. We will turn this responsibility over to them.' The responsibility was delegated to people who were acceptable both to the people and to the leaders. We do not need to see these seven men as the first diaconate. They were not given the titles deacons. They were simply commissioned to a particular work of service. There is a danger, I think, in some church circles of being over-simplistic about this and saying that there were two strands of leadership in the New Testament: elders and deacons. The elders looked after the spiritual matters and the deacons looked after the material. I do not think that is true. The Bible is always far more concerned with function rather than label or status.

They also delegated to the seven a recognized authority

in order to get the job done. They chose them, commissioned them and let them get on with it: 'They presented these men to the apostles, who prayed and laid their hands on them' (verse 6). When we commission people to do jobs in the church, one of the most vital principles is that we let them get on with it. In a growing church, there has to be a continual development of delegated authority. Otherwise we have a recipe for stagnation and bottlenecks.

This in turn led to renewed priorities: 'We will . . . give our attention to prayer and the ministry of the word' (verse 4). The apostles saw these as their primary responsibility. As a minister, I see that as my primary responsibility too and I think any local church pastor must be someone who gives himself to prayer and the ministry of the word. While there are many other things that clamour to be done, since organization is important, these matters are of supreme importance. We receive God's power through the prayer of faith and we use that power for his glory in the ministry of the word, because that is the divinely appointed means by which salvation comes to men and women and by which God's people are built up. Happy the church that allows its ministers to follow these priorities and happy the church that reflects that in the lives of its members. Where these are our primary concerns we shall see the life and power of God manifested.

The blessing of the crisis was that it led the whole church to reaffirm its priorities. So the word of God spread because there was unity, because there was love, because the problem had been effectively dealt with. And the witness of the church was authentic. The people's lives confirmed what they said and the number of the disciples increased rapidly. Satan's attempts to mar and spoil the church by the chuntering within were overruled by the Spirit of God for a much greater good. There was rapid growth and new areas began to be reached: 'a large number of priests became obedient to the faith' (verse 7). Who would have expected the priests to start responding to the gospel? That previously resistant area now began to open up, at least partly because God's people affirmed their priorities and because together they would let nothing divide them. The went on in love, in faith and with a commitment to prayer and the ministry of the word.

12

Solving Problems and Moving Forward

I have given the chapter this title because these two ingredients are never far apart from one another in church life. Church growth always produces its own problems and if forward momentum is to be maintained these problems have to be solved.

As the gospel spread in heathen cities, it was natural that the churches that were established were predominantly Gentile. They had little or no Jewish Old Testament background. We saw in the last chapter, looking at Acts 6, that in the early days of the Jerusalem church there was already developing a tension between the Aramaic-speaking and the Greek-speaking communities, in the case of the comparatively uncomplicated matter of the distribution of alms to the widows.

Now we come in chapter 15 of Acts to what I can only describe as a time bomb that had been smouldering increasingly as the gospel spread, but which we need to recognize was an issue that threatened to blow the whole of the young church to pieces. We are looking at a particular historical incident that, in the hands of God, became a means by which the gospel spread even more effectively. But let us not underestimate the devastating effect that might well have been produced had this problem not been solved as it was. Thus, as we take this historical passage, we recognize that the situation it describes is not unique. It is the continuing experience of the church that wherever there is expansion and growth, the enemy will always try to stop it, and often by internal disagreements and disputes among the believers. However, we also need to realize from a historical passage like this that we can learn biblical principles about how to deal with other matters that threaten to undermine our contemporary unity as Christians, whether it is within a local church or as a group of churches in a locality, or indeed in our wider groupings across the country.

The problem is stated at the end of Acts 14 and the start of Acts 15. The apostles were sent out by the church at Antioch, so they reported back to the whole church at the end of their missionary journey. This is in itself an important church principle. They were the instruments through whom God had worked, and the most amazing thing that had happened on this missionary journey was that God had opened the door of faith even to the Gentiles (Acts 14:27). The conversion of these Gentile people, in various cities, was something that was God's initiative. But the door he had opened, by which he brought them into his kingdom, was not the door of law-keeping but that of faith. That phrase is going to be very important when we come to chapter 15.

Acts 14:28 indicates that Paul and Barnabas continued there in the church at Antioch fulfilling the tasks they had before they were sent out on their missionary journey. But the situation had changed while they were away. The church was now a mixture of Jews, 'proselytes', and Gentiles. Some were Gentiles who had become Jews; these were known as the proselytes. Others were Gentiles who had been converted direct into the Christian church. Therefore the church at Antioch represented a new order, and a mixture of both Jewish and Gentile backgrounds. But the old order, the original Jewish church in Jerusalem, contained an influential group who were far from happy about these Gentile believers, who seemed not to submit to the law of Moses. So we find in verse 1 of Chapter 15 that this more extreme Jewish party in Jerusalem sends a representative delegation to launch a campaign for the law of Moses in the church at Antioch: 'Some men came down from Judea to Antioch and were teaching the brothers: "Unless you are circumcised according to the custom taught by Moses, you cannot be saved."' Their teaching was both clear and direct. The verb indicates that they set about it with some spirit and determination. So into this mixture of Jews and Gentiles you have now injected a little group of teachers from the mother church at Jerusalem who came and preached a message, which effectively said: 'No circumcision, no salvation. You cannot be a Christian unless you are circumcised according to the law of Moses.'

They were not arguing that Christians in the Gentile church should not associate with Jews—far from it—but that you could not become a full member of the community of Christ unless you came under the law of Moses and received its sign of circumcision. Certainly Gentiles could be admitted, but as far as these Jews were concerned it was not by the door of faith alone. It was the door of faith and the door of the law that had to be entered. That was clearly an absolutely basic issue that would affect the spread of the gospel through the whole Gentile world. It is important to remember that it challenged the very foundation of the apostolic mission. At this point in time, it would have been very easy for the church to split into Jewish and Gentile factions. That was the problem that they faced at Antioch.

Acts 15 has the story of how they explored it together. 'This brought Paul and Barnabas into sharp dispute and debate with them' (verse 2). They began vigorously to oppose the teaching that was coming from these Jerusalem brothers. Luke speaks literally of discord and not a little questioning. One can imagine the hours they took in trying to sort this out together, since it involved them in very detailed debate. The word used for discord here is one that is generally used in political contexts. It means irreconcilable differences and very deep divisions. Perhaps this was inevitable because so much was at stake. Paul was not simply going to say that this was just a difference of emphasis. He realized that if these people were going to win the church to their way of thinking, they would in fact undermine the gospel and because it was the gospel at stake—primary truth concerning how a man is made right with God—Paul resisted with everything in him this teaching which was being insinuated in the church by obviously Christian people from Jerusalem but men whom he considered to be seriously in error.

We have Paul's own account of the matter in the letter to the Galatians. The exact timing and the intricacies that Paul is describing is a little difficult to work out. However, it seems undoubtedly clear that it is this incident that he is thinking about when he says in Galatians 2:11,

> When Peter came to Antioch, I opposed him to his face, because he was in the wrong. Before certain men came from James, he used to eat with the Gentiles. But when they arrived he began to draw back and separate himself from the Gentiles because he was afraid of those who belonged to the circumcision group. The other Jews joined him in his hypocrisy, so that by their hypocrisy even Barnabas was led astray. When I saw that they were not acting in line with the truth of the gospel, I said to Peter in front of them all, 'You are a Jew, yet you live like a Gentile and not like a Jew. How is it, then, that you force Gentiles to follow Jewish customs?'

It may be that this happened at a different time from the incident in Acts 15. It may just have happened in a parallel situation, but it is significant that Peter was in Antioch, that his experience with Cornelius (Acts 10) was leading him to the same position as Paul, and that before these people came down from Jerusalem, Peter was apparently quite happy to eat with the Gentiles. He made no differences between them and certainly never insisted that Gentiles should follow the Jewish customs, until the party from Jerusalem came. They are described as being from James, not because they had that apostle's authorization (he denies that in Acts 15:24) but because he was the apostle at Jerusalem identified as the leader of the Jerusalem church. So Peter began to come under pressure from the legalistic Christians. He withdrew into what Paul denounces as 'hypocrisy'. The word literally means 'play acting'. There was a fundamental unreality about what he was doing in Antioch now. And the other Jewish Christians, and even Barnabas, that great encourager, were affected by it too. Paul had to rebuke them. He had to say to them that they were no longer acting in line with the truth of the gospel.

This must have had the desired effect on Peter, because he was certainly convinced of the rightness of Paul's thought. When he comes, later in Acts 15, to speak at the council in Jerusalem, what he says is very much in support of Paul's position. But the problem was beginning to affect the major leaders of the church. It was penetrating all that they were doing. It was not something that could be brushed under the carpet, but an issue that demanded a solution. Paul could so easily have gone his own way. We know that he was a Roman citizen, that he had largely rejected the pharisaism with which he had grown up. Why not separate off from the Jerusalem church with its bigotted legalistic attitudes? Why bother with these Jews who were insisting on the law of Moses? The temptation may well have been there, but he refused to travel that route. Instead, Paul and Barnabas were appointed, with other believers, to go to Jerusalem and discuss the whole matter with the apostles and the elders there. And, 'The church sent them on their way' (verse 3).

Their course of action follows the teaching of Jesus in Matthew 18:15–17, which we examined in an earlier chapter. It is a principle for personal relationships, but clearly it also applies to relationships within the churches. There should be a consultation first of all between the parties that are at variance. In this instance it applied to Paul and Barnabas and the men of Jerusalem. But if the issue could not be settled at that level, then provision was made for it to be dealt with in a wider forum. Paul and Barnabas were appointed to go up to the elders and apostles in Jerusalem. And eventually there had to be a meeting in Jerusalem of the whole church to decide it. The important factor was that at every stage there existed a willingness publicly to discuss and work through these issues, with a desire to resolve them. The thing that so often poisons Christian relationships is the unwillingness of individuals, or a group, to carry that out in a face-to-face context. The Antioch church was obviously very enthusiastic about this. They sent them on their way, which probably means they accompanied them part of the way. They provided the means by which they could travel, by paying their expenses.

As Paul and Barnabas travelled, they shared the good news of the Gentile conversions. It is significant, incidentally, that they shared it in Phoenicia and Samaria, but when they reached Judea, they have the sensitivity and tact not to do so. They were anxious not to exacerbate the situation. So this is how the problem is to be solved. There is to be a sorting out between the two groups, as they come together to discuss their understanding of God's word and God's actions. That is the Christian way to deal with it. 'When they came to Jerusalem, they were welcomed by the church and the apostles and elders, to whom they reported everything God had done through them' (verse 4).

Next, there was a general meeting of the church and we find those believers who were Pharisees putting forward their position (verse 5) that is, the Gentiles must be circumcised in order to keep the law of Moses which they are now required to obey. These Pharisees were evidently people who accepted Jesus as Messiah, but who retained their old legalism. The discussion is not allowed to continue in open forum. Having raised the matter with the whole church, the apostles and elders first of all met *in camera* to consider the question (verse 6). There was a special meeting of the leaders of the churches, Jerusalem and Antioch. It was a lengthy debate (verse 7) and there was much discussion and questioning necessary to establish all the facts and arguments. Only then could they make a right decision, and move forward in a frank and open way. It should hardly be necessary to comment that it is essential when we are trying to come to agreement on areas of difficulty that there should be a clear stating of the issues. Yet so often this vital part of the process is omitted.

Next, Luke gives the substance of the three most crucial contributions to the debate. Peter's contribution is recorded in verse 7–11, Barnabas' and Paul's in verse 12 and James' in verses 13–21. Peter takes a very brave, uncompromising stand. It is by now probably about ten years since the conversion of Cornelius (Acts 10). At first, Peter had not been able to believe that he was being sent to a Gentile centurion. But eventually he followed God's command and went to Cornelius. To his amazement, the centurion and his household trusted the Lord and were filled with the Holy Spirit. Notice in Peter's speech, which is summarized here, that all his reasoning is based on what God has done. There are four important verbs: 'Brothers, you know that . . . God made a choice' (verse 7)—God chose that the Gentiles might hear the gospel; 'God . . . showed that he accepted them by giving the Holy Spirit to them' (verse 8); 'He [God] made no distinction between us and them' (verse 9); 'He [God] purified their hearts' (verse 9). God chose, God gave the Spirit, God did not distinguish, God cleansed their hearts.

Now if God had done all that, said Peter, who are you to resist him? God chose Peter to preach the good news to this group of Gentiles so that they might believe and be saved. They were all talking about the vision he had received and how he really needed convincing that he had to go to the Gentiles. But it was God who brought Cornelius and Peter together, without any human planning. It was transparently a work of God's sovereign grace. And as Peter preached Jesus to them, the Holy Spirit came upon them, as a witness to their being received into the community of Christians. What the Jerusalem church had received, they too received from God's hand, by his direct intervention, so that no one could doubt that God had accepted these people and made them Christians. There was no difference at all, said Peter, between us and them. He cleansed their hearts, by faith, as he did ours. God made no distinctions.

So Peter used what God had done and the evident signs of God's work among the Gentiles as his way into the problem and said, in effect, 'This is the proof that God is at work in these people's lives. But the transformation has come about not through circumcision, but by faith. They are just as much forgiven as we are. Why then try to test God by putting on the necks of these disciples the yoke that neither we nor our fathers were able to bear? If God has done this and receives these people why should other Christians distrust his guidance or try to disobey his clearly revealed will? Peter's challenge to his fellow Jews is whether they are going to submit to God or follow their own prejudice. Will they insist on their tradition and their law-keeping, or are they going to move within God's revealed will? That is the question he opens up to them.

In pursuing this argument, Peter reminded his Jewish listeners that none of their fathers could ever keep the law, even though they were Jews by birth. It was a heavy yoke and none of them were able to bear it. In contrast, the yoke of the Lord Jesus is easy and his burden is light, because our salvation is not by a supreme effort of law-keeping, but by faith, through grace. Christ has opened the door of faith to the Gentiles and as you go through it, by God's grace, you are justified, accepted and brought into membership of God's new covenant people. This point is stressed in verse 11: 'We believe it is through the grace of our Lord Jesus that we are saved, just as they are.' Jews and Gentiles—one door of salvation, one work of grace, one way into the kingdom, through faith in Christ alone.

We too must grasp that. People today are not saved by faith in Jesus through the grace of God *and* keeping the particular evangelical traditions of our churches. It is by grace *alone*, through faith, that men and women are saved. As evangelical Christians, with a very high view of the authority of Scripture, we face a similar problem to that which beset the Pharisees. They too held the strongest views about the reliability of God's word, but subtly and almost without realizing it, they allowed their interpretations of Scripture and their additional traditions, sincerely built on Scripture as they saw it, to assume an equivalent authority as the pure word of God itself. This is always a danger for those who have a comprehensive written authority. The answer is not to dispense with the authority of Scripture, but to be especially careful and watchful for the incipient danger of making our own traditions the touchstone by which other people are to be accepted by God. This is the danger about which Peter is so forcefully warning them.

Neither Peter nor any Bible teacher would want to deny that there are certain obvious ways in which people reveal the reality of their Christian mission. True Christians delight in keeping the principles of God's law. They will want to be those who live out the law in their lives. But equally, they do not seek to keep the law as the means by which they were blessed. God's goodness to us is all undeserved. It is pure grace. Yet we so easily fall into this trap. We think that if only we can keep the law of God, then we shall be worthy of God's blessing. So although our whole Christian experience declares that we are justified by faith, and we accept that in our minds, in practice we are frequently going on as Christians by our own unaided efforts, struggling terribly hard to keep the law of God and finding that we cannot do it. Whereas the Bible says we are justified solely by the grace of God, through Jesus. Our keeping of God's law, which he does require because he wants us to live a life pleasing to him and therefore according to his standards, can only happen as we respond to that grace of God. It is that grace that enables us to live lives that are increasingly like the Lord Jesus.

To some this may seem an oversubtle distinction, but actually it makes all the difference in living the Christian life. If it is you struggling hard to keep the law of God, you will fail over and over again. But if you receive the grace of God freshly every day and say, 'Lord, I cannot be the person you want me to be, but you can live that life through me and you can change me into the image of Christ. It is through grace that I have been saved; it is through grace that I am living; it is by faith in you that I claim the power of your Spirit to live a life that will be different,' then your life will be pleasing to God. But not the other way round. All around the world you will find Christians who are still trying to grapple with this key issue. It is through grace we are saved by faith. Peter expressed it very penetratingly. He saw, having come from a Jewish background, that if this was not accepted as the foundation of the gospel and the condition of its progress, the whole forward movement of the church would be impeded.

It is no wonder that the apostles and elders were silent (verse 12) as they listened to Barnabas and Paul, who did not attack the false view from a theological perspective. Paul, the great theologian, told of what had happened in his experience; miraculous acts of God that had confirmed his work among the Gentiles. These were further remarkable evidences indicating that God had been pleased to accept these people into his kingdom. Perhaps he felt that Peter had already done the job theologically! As they had travelled from city to city, Paul and Barnabas had seen Gentiles being converted. They were already in God's kingdom, fully accepted by him. How could men require them, in addition, to be circumcised? They were already their brothers.

Then James, the apostle in residence at Jerusalem, brings the debate to a conclusion. His summing up was as the leader of the Jerusalem church, as one who commanded the support of the pharasaical party and as one whom Paul also acknowledged. Notice that he used Peter's Aramaic name, Simon, revealing his Jewish culture and origin. James concluded that this new revelation of God accorded with his written revelation in the Old Testament scriptures, what we might call the biblical norm. Once more, the litmus paper by which everything must be assessed is what Scripture teaches. Here he goes back to the Old Testament prophet, Amos, but significantly, he quotes from the Septuagint, the Greek version of the text, not the Hebrew version. You would have expected James, as a Jew, to use the Hebrew Scriptures, but he does not. The Masoretic text, the Hebrew version, talks not about the remnant of men, in verse 16, but 'the remnant of Edom'. The difference is a technical one, relating to the pointing of the text. According to which vowels were used, the verse can mean either the remnant of Edom or the remnant of Adam, that is the remnant of men. The Septuagint reading took it as the remnant of men, thus opening the gospel up for the Gentile world. The very significant fact is that James took the Greek version and he used that instead, because his heart was so opened to these Gentile Christians. He was always prepared to recognize what God was doing in other people's lives. He pointed out that God had always purposed to bring in Gentiles: 'that have been known for ages' (verse 18). When you read the Old Testament you cannot escape the fact that God is not just interested in the Jews. All along, his concern is for the Gentiles as well, for every human being created in his image. So what is to be done? The leader of the Jerusalem church, to whom these Pharisees were responsible, concludes that they must not put unnecessary obstacles in the way, nor impose extra yokes on the Gentiles. They must not impose conditions for salvation or Christian fellowship on them, other than the faith in Christ that they had already demonstrated.

That is the great principle that is established here. Once it is accepted it follows that all the church needs to do is to write a tolerant, courteous letter to their Gentile brothers, asking them to respect certain Jewish food scruples, to have done with idols, and to keep God's commandments concerning sexual morality. But, he said, we are not going to demand that they are circumcised. We will not make them into Jews for we accept them as Christians. The Law of Moses has been well-known in the Gentile communities and those who are free from it should not offend the consciences of their Jewish brothers. But on the other hand, the Jewish brothers must not compel them to keep that law in all its detail, because very much of that law, particularly its ceremonial aspects, has been fulfilled in Christ, and it has been folded up and put away as part of the Old Covenant.

We do not have space in this book to go into the relationship between the law and grace. But one can see here in its limited context how these actions were used by the Spirit to bring renewed unity. They went back to the Scriptures and so they established the priorities of the gospel. Building on those revealed principles, they were able to recognize one another as fellow believers, courteously to respect one another, to bear with one another and to encourage and strengthen one another in their common faith.

Let me finish by outlining these principles, which form a pattern for dealing with differences within the church of God.

(1) There was open discussion among the believers of all the issues that would threaten their unity. You find that in verses 2, 4, 6 and 12. Open frank discussion of whatever threatens unity is the number-one principle.

(2) They identified their personal prejudices and then separated them from God's guidance, by specifically researching what God was doing in other people's lives (verse 7–11). That is what James is doing in his summing up. Responding to the evidence presented by Peter and Paul, he puts on one side his own background, recognizes what God is doing, and accepts it as a gospel principle.

(3) They tested everything by the Scriptures (verse 14–18).

(4) They refused to compromise on the essentials of the gospel. It was the good news of Christ's salvation that bound them together (verses 2, 11 and 19). Therefore, they would not compromise it, whatever changes in thinking that required or dictated.

(5) In other areas, that were not primary gospel areas, they respected one another's scruples. They were willing to be conciliatory, because they loved one another, in Christ, and they wanted to encourage one another. That was the eventual outcome of this exercise.

When the delegates returned to the church in Antioch, they gathered it together, read the letter from the Christians in Jerusalem and met with a glad response. The ambassadors from Jerusalem, far from putting them under the yoke of the law, encouraged and strengthened the brothers (verse 32), so that when they had spent some time preaching and teaching, 'they were sent off by the brothers with the blessing of peace to return to those who had sent them' (verse 33). What had begun as a sharp dispute and a potentially devisive debate ended with the blessing of peace. It is a marvellous testimony to the work of the Spirit of love and joy. It is also a thrilling testimony to the willingness of the church to be led by God and not by their own prejudices. Why? Because the gospel was central. There was no compromise concerning the grounds on which a man is made right with God, but their genuine Christian love held that truth in sympathy, compassion, and above all in understanding. May God grant us grace to solve our church problems in that way and so to keep moving forward.

13

What Jesus Wants His Church to Be

There can be few more encouraging and comforting words that you can say to anyone, or that you can hear said to you, than the words, 'I shall be praying for you.' Prayer is the most valuable activity we can be involved in on someone else's behalf. Yet all too often we promise to pray, but somehow we forget to do so, or we pray about a matter once and then it slips from our minds. I wonder if you know that the Lord Jesus is himself praying for you. He is the one who speaks to the Father on our behalf, as our advocate in heaven (1 Jn 2:1). His intercession is the guarantee of our full salvation, for 'he is able to save completely those who come to God through him, because he always lives to intercede for them' (Heb 7:25). Jesus prays for us individually, so that it is through him we are able to approach God's throne and make our needs known to him. But he also prays for the church. He prays for each of us personally and also for us corporately, and that is what the closing words of John 17 are all about. They are the prayer that Jesus prays for his church:

> My prayer is not for them [the disciples] alone. I pray also for those who will believe in me through their message, that all

of them may be one, Father, just as you are in me and I am in you. May they also be in us so that the world may believe that you have sent me. I have given them the glory that you gave me, that they may be one as we are one: I in them and you in me. May they be brought to complete unity to let the world know that you sent me and have loved them even as you have loved me. Father, I want those you have given me to be with me where I am, and to see my glory, the glory you have given me because you loved me before the creation of the world. Righteous Father, though the world does not know you, I know you, and they know that you have sent me. I have made you known to them, and will continue to make you known in order that the love you have for me may be in them and that I myself may be in them (Jn 17:20–26).

In this historical account of the prayer Jesus offered to his Father on the night of his betrayal, there are two great requests that he is making for his church; not just the infant church that was about to be born, through the cross and the resurrection, but for the church in every generation. You will find the first in verse 21: 'That all of them may be one.' And the second request is in verse 24: 'Father, I want those you have given me to be with me where I am.' Together, they articulate the Saviour's will for his church throughout history. Jesus is praying for a spiritual unity among all God's people, based upon our individual union with Christ. These verses have a great deal to teach us, especially in this age when, in spite of all the talk about Christian unity, there is still so comparatively little real expression of it.

I wonder if you ever ask yourself the question, 'Does it really matter that the Christian church is divided?' Ought we to be praying, as some have suggested, 'Lord, forgive us our denominations?' I am reminded of the story of a little boy, who was the son of a very active worker in a local church. Because there was no settled minister in the church, the family would often have a visiting preacher

home to lunch with them. On one celebrated occasion, as
yet another visitor came through the door, the little boy
sighed and said to him, 'And what abomination do you
belong to?' The visiting preacher, who was well up to this,
replied, 'Well, I am a methylated Baptist.' I don't know
whether you have problems explaining to people what
'abomination' you belong to, but certainly denominational
labels should never be barriers to fellowship among believers, from how many different backgrounds, who are
all one in Christ Jesus. But what does Jesus have to teach
us about spiritual unity? I want to point out several
important factors briefly from these verses.

Firstly, spiritual unity is a unity of believers. 'My prayer
is not for them alone. I pray also for those who will believe
in me through their message' (verse 20). Jesus is telling us
in this prayer that *the fundamental ground of all Christian
unity is belief in him*; faith in Christ, as Saviour and Lord.
He further identifies it as believing in him 'through their
message', the gospel message to be carried by the apostles
whom he had just finished praying for. So the ground of
unity is a common faith in Christ, through the apostolic
message. There is no other way by which a person can
become a Christian, but by receiving the truth of the
gospel handed down from those original apostles who
were listening to Jesus' prayer. They were there as Jesus
was praying, listening to what he was saying, and they
were the men who became the custodians of his message.
That message was Jesus himself. So wherever they went
they proclaimed him, and other people began to believe in
Jesus through that message, which they fearlessly
preached.

For the first Christians, it was the preaching of these
disciples, who were there with Jesus as he prayed, that
brought them to believe in him. For us, who cannot go
and listen to the apostle Peter, or the apostle John preach,
it is the apostolic truth recorded in the Bible, under the

inspiration of the Holy Spirit, preserved through the centuries and translated into our own language, as the written word of God. How frequently we should remember with thanksgiving those who gave their lives so that we might have the Scriptures in our own language. Paul said to the Roman Christians, 'faith comes from hearing the message, and the message is heard through the word of Christ' (Rom 10:17). What he meant was that if anyone wants to know Jesus Christ personally, they will find him in the Scriptures. Study the Bible, soak yourself in the Bible, let the Bible speak to you every day, and it will not be long before you find Jesus for yourself, because the Bible is God's ordained means of bringing people to spiritual life. That is why it is the only source book for our message, unparalleled by any other book in the history of mankind. It is the message of Jesus, who can change your life, who can come into your experience to make you clean and give you his power to transform you and to send you out into the world for him as you bring his love to other people.

The Bible is the ultimate authority. The church stands upon the truth of God in the Scriptures, not upon its own traditions, not upon our reasoning processes, not upon our personal experience of Christ, rich though they all may be, but upon the word of God, upon the rock of Scripture. That is the only foundation on which we can build securely, and Jesus himself, the living word, is the message of the written word. So we meet Christ when we read in the Bible the record of the historical events by which God acted in our world, in Jesus, and the divine explanation and interpretation of those events, both of which are the contents of the Bible.

So, Jesus says that it is of crucial importance if we are to understand the nature of true spiritual unity, that we see it as a unity of believers. Believers in Jesus who are committed to him personally and who know that his word is the truth in an ultimate and absolute sense, are one in Christ. Whatever label a person may choose to wear is comparatively unimportant, if that person is someone committed to Jesus Christ in a faith relationship, through the apostolic message. And if an individual has not yet been brought to confess that Jesus Christ is Lord, in a personal, life-changing way, which means living under his authority, then whatever label they may wear, Jesus denies that person the right to be called a Christian. The issue that matters is whether or not you confess that Jesus Christ is Lord. Are you living your life under his authority? Is he actually in the driving seat of your life? That is what it means to be a Christian, and it is that one faith in Christ that unites all his people.

The corollary of that is that we must never allow other ingredients to separate us. There are Christians who believe in the Lord Jesus as he is portrayed in the Scriptures, who trust him, love him and seek to follow him, who can nevertheless disagree about other secondary matters. They may disagree about church government; about whether church leaders should be elected or appointed, about whether they should be individual to one church or diocesan. They may disagree about styles of worship, about whether to have an organ or not, about whether to have an orchestra or not, about whether to sing choruses or hymns, about whether to put your hands up or keep them down. There are all sorts of different styles of worship, which often simply reflect our cultural likes or dislikes, but we are not to be separated by those things. Bible Christians recognize that there is unity far deeper than church government, styles of worship or denominational labels, for we are all one in Christ Jesus (Gal 3:28) if we truly believe in him and if our lives are governed by his message.

Spiritual unity then is unity of believers. There is a given unity among all who are born again by God's Spirit, which nothing can destroy. There is a oneness in Christ that unites the members of God's family whatever their church tradition, in their confession that Jesus Christ is Lord, and a resolve to practise his lordship under the authority of his word.

The second quality to notice about true spiritual unity is that it is a unity with God. In verse 21, Jesus prays that 'all of them may be one, Father, just as you are in me and I am in you. May they also be in us so that the world may believe that you have sent me.' So, the model pattern of Christian unity is that deep union between the Father and Son. But it is one of the deepest mysteries of the Bible, how the Son on earth and the Father in heaven could be one. We know that the closeness of union between Jesus, the Son of God on earth, and his Father in heaven was the common life that was in them.

Although Jesus Christ was man, we know too that he was nothing less than God. The life of God was his life. He was not God dressed up in human clothes, as though he were not truly man; nor was he a man who although greatly inspired, was not truly God. In Christ, the two natures were both divine and human, combined forever in the one person. He was and is both truly God and truly man. The life of God was within Jesus. This means that there never was a time when Jesus did not exist; from before the creation of the world he was, because he is God from everlasting. Moreover, there never was a time when he was not God. Always, he was the eternal Son of the everlasting Father.

We cannot begin to get our minds around this, but we do start to understand something of its meaning when we remember that the life of God came, in the person of the Lord Jesus, into our world of time and space. He came to show us what God is like and to make it clear to us that there is a God and that Jesus is his exact representation in humanity (Heb 1:3). The amazing thing that verse 21 says is that this life of God is to be within every individual Christian as a personal experience: 'May they also be in us'. Who are 'they'? Clearly, they are the Christians who are going to believe in him, including you and me. Who is 'us'? The Father, the Son and the Holy Spirit, united in the Trinity. Jesus says, therefore, that spiritual unity is unity with God, or, deeper than that, it is a unity *in* God. If you are a Christian, you are in Christ, in the Father and the Son, and that means that the life of God flows into you and through you into the world.

Someone who lives in God has the same desires that God has. Christians long to win a lost world back to God, because that is their Father's heart. Someone who is living in God is becoming more and more like him, in a life of love and holiness. Wherever you go in the world, wherever you meet other believers, you can recognize the family likeness, so that however different you may be, in all sorts of ways, there is still a depth of fellowship and unity that has no other explanation than that you share the same life. You are one in Christ because you both know and love the same Saviour. Therefore, spiritual unity is not achieved by commissions, synods or committees; it is achieved by the Holy Spirit in each one of God's children, knitting our hearts together in love and uniting our minds in God's truth. It is a unity with God.

'I have given them the glory that you gave me, that they may be one as we are one' Jesus continues (verse 22). If the pattern of unity in the second half of the verse is that we may be one as the Father and the Son are one in the Godhead, then that means that we have got to get on with one another, doesn't it? The beginning of verse 23 says it again: 'I in them and you in me.' If Jesus lives in us, then we are united through him to the Father and that means we are really one body with every other true Christian around the world. One church, one faith, one Lord, one mind, one will, one heart, one judgement, although we are many members. Nor can we see that unity completely manifested in any individual local church, even if it is a megachurch in California with 20,000 members. You see it only in the whole body of Christ, throughout the whole world. This is a unity that nothing can create and nothing can destroy.

We do not, however, have to seek uniformity; that is to miss the point. Christ's petition does not imply that all Christians should be carbon copies of one another. One of the marks of the sub-Christian cults is that they tend to produce people who are exactly the same. You go through the machinery and you come out at the end conditioned, trained and exactly the same as the next person, like so many articles off an assembly line. In contrast, it is a mark of the reality of the gospel that Christians are vastly different from one another. There is an enormous and glorious variety within the church of God, reflecting our Maker who created a physical world in which variety is so prevalent. Just look at the natural order of the world with its many, many glorious creations: all sorts of things, powerful, tiny, beautiful; and its vast array of colours, which man cannot imitate. That is what the church is like too, with its 'all sorts and conditions of men'. But there is a unity among all true believers who are in Christ in every church and every denomination. And we can agree to differ on the secondary matters, on the relatively peripheral things, because we have a fundamental unity that is in Jesus. We do not all have to do exactly the same things as all the other Christians.

If the Lord Jesus prayed for that unity, then I must do nothing to break it. I must not shake that oneness, but be eager to preserve it. So I want to have fellowship on earth with every brother and sister I meet, with whom, by God's grace, I shall one day be in heaven. I believe that that is the sort of unity that God is looking for and praying for among his people. We need to value and cultivate truly evangelical unity in the gospel much more actively and enthusiastically than has been the case in recent years. We may differ from one another about baptism, or bishops, or about forms of service, or about gifts of the Spirit, or about any other secondary matters which are not fundamental to the gospel. But I am not going to separate myself from those who disagree with me on certain things into some narrow, introverted group that simply dots all their 'i's and crosses all their 't's as I do. We are one in Christ and we have an obligation to express the biblical unity. As evangelical Christians, we do not have the option of separating ourselves out from other members of God's family who do not see things in quite the same way as we do. There is a biblical unity for which Christ is praying, and which I, for one, long to see in much more practical ways throughout the church in our land at this time. There have been far too many walls built between Bible-believing Christians over secondary matters. Those walls need to be knocked down. We need to recognize that we are one in Christ. Spiritual unity is a unity of believers and a unity with God.

Thirdly, it is a unity for the world. Look at the end of verse 21 again: 'May they also be in us so that the world may believe that you have sent me.' Jesus is saying that the spiritual unity of Christians has an evangelistic effect. When the world sees Christians as one, the result, Jesus says, is that the world will believe that the Father has sent him. Too often we Bible Christians have ignored that and we need to repent of it. When the world sees Christians behaving as they sometimes do, quarrelling and divided from one another, defensive and critical of others, what do they conclude? The world judges that our gospel is a fiction. It cannot be real, because it does not work. We cannot even agree among ourselves. I am convinced that one of the main reasons for the low ebb of spiritual life in Western Europe in recent decades has been the divisions that exist between true believers across the continent. Of course, no externally contrived union will ever convince unbelievers, however clever and impressive a human structure it may be. But where there is a spiritual union with one Master, one message and one mission, the Lord Jesus himself says that that will convince the world that the Father really did send his Son to save us. Why is that? Surely, because the world then sees the message that Jesus taught and lived being worked out in the lives of those who claim to follow him. It is these ordinary human beings transformed by the power of Christ.

That needs to be worked out at every level. Take, for example, the individual level. Suppose I go into work tomorrow and I behave in a thoroughly worldly way as though I were not a Christian. By this I do not mean I commit some gross sin, but I am snappy with people, critical about my fellow Christians and pick holes in what is going on in my church. What I communicate is that I have no care or love for those with whom I am supposed to be as one. If that is my lifestyle, then I need not expect my colleagues to be interested at lunch-time about what I was doing on Sunday, because I have already denied any verbal witness I might give by the way I have behaved on Monday. The world is looking to see a Christianity that is authentic and made real by its love.

It needs to be true at the family level too. If, in a Christian family, the talk at the table is often critical of other Christians, if it is taking to bits what is going on in the church and saying this is wrong and that is wrong, do not expect the children in that family to grow up believing that Christianity is true, because the family is continually denying it. Where is the love, or the sympathy, or the understanding we profess should be there?

Similarly, in a local church, if the Christians in that part of the body are always at one another, falling out with one another, and not able to agree together, of course the people around are not going to queue up to come within the orbit of that church's life. Why should they? The unspoken message of the church's behaviour is that what we say with our lips we do not intend to practise in our lives. In the nation, if Bible-believing Christians do not get together, pray and work together, at every opportunity that they have, then the unbelieving nation says, 'They don't *really* believe it, because it doesn't really work, even for them.' I'm not talking about ecumenical gatherings. I'm not saying that there can be a unity between people who claim to be Christians but deny the deity of Christ or his bodily resurrection. As we have seen, only the truth of the apostolic gospel is an adequately firm foundation. But where that foundation exists, why are we so happy to allow barriers to remain between us? I believe we do need to repent of our unnecessary divisions, which often owe more to our pride and prejudice than to God's truth, and to ask him to forgive us.

If you are at school, college or university you need to identify with the other Christians there, so that you are seen to be one body in that place for God, to make an impact on your community. Perhaps there is a Christian Union in the place where you work. Are you involved in it and praying for it? Are you united with the Christians who are your colleagues there? Maybe there is a house-group that meets for prayer and Bible study in your area. Are you prepared to meet with them and pray for your joint outreach into that area, so that you are seen to be one body in Christ, in your little bit of God's earth?

Real heart unity between believers shakes the world because there is nothing like it anywhere else in human society. Where you find a group of Christians who love one another and are united to one another you will find something that is unique to the church. The world cannot begin to copy that in any way. But, similarly, divisions among true believers are the greatest possible injury to the cause of the gospel. If ever you are tempted to break up the unity of a church or a group of Christians, consider it well. You may be doing the greatest damage to the gospel that you could possibly do. You may be causing little ones to stumble, and Jesus said it is better to have a millstone hung around your neck and to be drowned in the depths of the sea than to do that (Mt 18:6) You may be destroying God's temple, and as Paul says in 1 Corinthians 3:17, if anyone destroys God's temple, God will destroy him. If the Lord Jesus is praying for unity, how *dare* we fight against that, whether it is in the church, or any other fellowship of Christians, or any other sort of context into which God sends us? True spiritual unity is powerfully evangelistic; it is a unity for the world to see.

Fourthly, it is a unity in glory: 'Father, I want those you have give me to be with me where I am, and to see my glory, the glory you have given me because you loved me before the creation of the world' (verse 24). Jesus wants his people to be with him. It is a wonderfully strengthening thought to know that his will, expressed in his praying, is that we shall go to be with him. As we struggle on, down here, he is looking forward to our arrival in his presence. And when that moment comes, and we see him face to face, we shall see his glory, as the outshining of his character. We shall share it, we shall be part of it. If that is something that the Son desires, then we know it is something that the Father will grant—a unity in glory. Heaven is the immediate, unhindered presence of Jesus. Here he describes it as to be with him where he is. I do not need any other definition for heaven than that— to be with Jesus where he is. No more distance, no more absence, for ever with the Lord, and for ever with those who have gone before us. We shall look on his face, share in his joy, praise his love and rejoice in his salvation. We shall be one in that glory which has always been his.

It was the unique glory of the cross that he was just

about to face and endure, and by grace that atoning death opened the door to glory for every one of us, as we trust in him. What a wonderful salvation this is! One with Christ on earth, we shall be one with him eternally and his glory will be ours. But that gives an urgent compulsion to the necessity for us to work this out here and now. It will never be perfect in this world, but we have to be actively working at it. If it is to be real there, it must start to be real here. It is no good talking about glory if in our lives here we are actually denying its substance. But anything we give up for him and for the prospect of glory is worth it. There is a unity in glory, to which God is going to bring us. God grant that we do not arrive shame-faced, because we were so disunited on earth, or so unwilling to let him bring us together.

Lastly, it is a unity of love. In spite of all Jesus has done, he has to say in verse 25 that the world still does not know him nor does it know his Father: 'Righteous Father, though the world does not know you, I know you, and they [the disciples] know that you have sent me. I have made you known to them, and will continue to make you known in order that the love you have for me may be in them and that I myself may be in them' (verses 25 and 26). Chapter 18 will illustrate very starkly the fact that the world does not know Jesus and cannot know God, as it shows us all sorts of people turning against him, because they do not know God. It is only through Jesus that you can come to the Father. By contrast, Jesus says the disciples have come to know who God is, through him. And everyone who has believed that message down the centuries has come to know him too. We can put ourselves into this, at the end of verse 25. We know that the Father sent Jesus, not because we are superior to others intellectually or spiritually, but because God has opened our eyes to see it. We know that the Father sent the Son to be the Saviour of the world (1 Jn 4:14). We understand that the great purpose of Jesus in his ministry was to reveal that Father, so as to bring men and women into a personal knowledge of God, which is eternal life (Jn 17:3). Now he promises that he will continue to do just that in the world: 'I . . . will continue to make you known in order that the love you have for me may be in them' (verse 26). While the primary reference must be to the cross, which was so soon to reveal the glory of Jesus to the fullest earthly extent, as he was lifted up to die, yet there is another sense in which whenever he is lifted up, by the preaching of the cross, he continues to reveal the Father's love, in every generation and throughout the world.

It was for this reason that the risen, victorious Lord gave his Holy Spirit to the church. He wants us to know the love that exists in God, in our own lives—the love of the Father through the Son, channelled to us by the Spirit. So, as the Spirit lives within us, he brings the love of Jesus into the deepest recesses of our personality and experience. It is the most wonderful thing in the world to know that you are loved by God and to know that every Christian is loved equally. For the love that the Father had for the Son is the very love by which he loves us, every one of us, whether we regard ourselves as experienced, mature Christians (who have perhaps forgotten how much we still have to learn) or as very young, weak and ineffective Christians (who have perhaps forgotten how far God has brought us). His love is great enough to reach every one of us, because it is the very same love that the Father had for Jesus that he has for us today, as his redeemed children. We are all the favourites, the special treasure, of the God who loves us and who lives within us.

That is the wonderful assurance contained in those amazing words at the end of the verse: ' . . . that I myself may be in them.' Jesus himself, in us—that is what it means to be a Christian. Nothing else, in all the world, can bring you joy, or peace, or fulfilment like that, and

Jesus is praying that we may know that as the deepest reality of our lives. For when that love is active in our lives, then it will be expressed in a widening love which God will give us for other people too. That love transcends, whether we like them or not. It is a love that goes out to them, a love that cares, and prays, builds up and strengthens. And the world will see its reality by the quality of oneness between God's people.

There is a unity of believers, which is grounded in God. It is a unity for the world to see, a unity which will one day find its completion in glory; but here and now it is a unity of Christian love, which is unlike any other quality of human life. If, in the closing hours of his earthly ministry Jesus made this desire the great substance of his prayer, should we not make its fulfilment the great passion of our lives?

14

The Bottom Line

I have never been very good at answering those penetrating questions usually phrased in superlatives, that are the stock-in-trade of interviewers: 'What was the most fulfilling, or embarrassing, or disappointing moment of your life?' Or that stultifying question on *Desert Island Discs*: 'What *one* luxury would you take with you?' I suppose the value of such questions is, as Dr Johnson put it 'to focus the mind wonderfully', though in his case he attributed this quality to the knowledge that one is about to be hanged! For those of us whose thinking has perennially fuzzy edges, or who are accustomed to infinitely variant shades of grey, rather than black and white, such questions do have a value. Similarly, at the end of our wide-ranging studies on the church, it is good to ask ourselves, what should the ultimate focus be, what is the bottom line? 'If there were just one quality we should seek to cultivate in our church life, what should it be?' Or, to put it another way, 'What is the most important priority for which Christ is looking in his church, in our generation?' The Bible provides a very clear answer.

To the angel of the church in Ephesus write: These are the

words of him who holds the seven stars in his right hand and walks among the seven golden lampstands: I know your deeds, your hard work and your perseverance. I know that you cannot tolerate wicked men, that you have tested those who claim to be apostles but are not, and have found them false. You have persevered and have endured hardships for my name, and have not grown weary. Yet I hold this against you: You have forsaken your first love. Remember the height from which you have fallen! Repent and do the things you did at first. If you do not repent, I will come to you and remove your lampstand from its place. But you have this in your favour: You hate the practices of Nicolaitans, which I also hate. He who has an ear, let him hear what the Spirit says to the churches. To him who overcomes I will give the right to eat from the tree of life, which is in the paradise of God (Rev 2:1–7).

The Book of Revelation begins with a vision of the Ascended Christ in glory, in unimaginable splendour:

His head and hair were white like wool, as white as snow, and his eyes were like blazing fire. His feet were like bronze glowing in a furnace, and his voice was like the sound of rushing waters . . . His face was like the sun shining in all its brilliance (Rev 1:14–16).

The exalted Lord is seen by John walking among seven golden lampstands which we are told symbolized the seven churches who are about to be addressed (1:20). As John fell at his feet as though dead, he received the reviving touch of Christ and the assurance that he who is alive for ever holds the keys of death and all that lies beyond.

The book continues with the seven letters to the churches, of which this to Ephesus is the first. Here we are face to face with the Lord of love, as he speaks so searchingly to his people in that congregation. Ephesus had been the focus of many blessings from his hand. Paul himself had ministered in the synagogue for three months and then in the school of Tyrannus for two years, during which the church had become a great missionary centre for the whole province of Asia. It is now about thirty-five years later. In the church at Ephesus, outwardly everything was in working order. The church continued her life. There was no failure in doctrine or in activity. But the Lord of the church had something against her: 'You have forsaken your first love' (2:4b). I cannot help wondering whether that is not what the one who walks among the churches would say about what he discovers in our congregations today. The primary application is to a local church and we must not forget that, but we all affect one another and we all have responsibilities for one another, as we have so often seen in the course of this book. In that all of our churches are made up of individual Christians, just like us, we need to take the relevance of this message to our own lives as well as to our corporate fellowship. It is largely the health of the local churches that determines the progress of the work of God in any locality or nation. How we respond to Christ's message here will have an impact far more widely in our own traditional lives or our own local circles.

In verse 2 and 3 we see the church that Christ knows. There are two impressive ingredients in these verses. The first is the Lord's infallible knowledge of his people: 'I know you deeds, your hard work and your perseverance'. The second is the quality of his church at Ephesus which he commends. If we had been invited to visit such a church I think in all probability you would have sung its praises and brought back a report on how fruitful and faithful it really was. We can only know in part because we only see in part. 'Man looks at the outward appearance, but the Lord looks at the heart' (1 Sam 16:7). Yet how many of the qualities of verses 2 and 3 are the very things we long to see in our churches and in our own lives? These were active, hard-working Christians. They toiled and laboured in Christ's service. They were not offering the Lord the ends of their spare time. Whatever it cost, they devoted themselves to his service. Nor was this something that only occurred in sporadic bursts. Christ himself notes their perseverance, commending them that their commitment to him was no sudden enthusiasm that faded when the going got difficult. There was a dependability about the discipleship of Ephesus. They were always on active service, come wind, come weather.

In addition, their ethical standards were high. There was no compromise with the surrounding pagan culture in matters of personal morality. This is the point the risen Lord is making in verse 6 when he refers to the practices of the Nicolaitans. Although there is some uncertainty as to what exactly that group believed and how they behaved, it seems most likely that they were a sect who taught that as we are saved by the free grace of God, it does not much matter what we do with our bodies, or with our lives in this world. Their false thinking centred on a separation of law from grace and of the flesh from the spirit. The attractiveness of their position was that they were able to lower God's standards, in order to accommodate their own sinfulness. But the Ephesian church had nothing to do with these things. Their standards of practical holiness were high.

The same thing is true of the church's doctrinal standards. They had taken care to test the teaching they had received and were not slow to repudiate what was false. Indeed, they had exercised discipline and maintained the purity of their faith. The teaching given and received within the congregation at Ephesus was thoroughly biblical and sound. When false teachers had arrived claiming a pseudo-apostolic authority for themselves, the church had rejected these claims and turned their back upon the teachings. Moreover, they had weathered the storm of persecution and had kept true to the Lord. In all this, they had not given up or grown tired; they were unswervingly faithful to Christ and to Christ's truth (verse 3). Who would not want to belong to a church like that? Who would not like to be that sort of Christian? And yet, after all this had been said, Christ held something against them. The bottom line is that permeating all these strengths, there was a hidden weakness that would ultimately ruin everything, like a crack in a building that eventually brings the whole structure to collapse.

After the commendations of verses 2 and 3, we must notice the charge that Christ makes (verse 4). It is significant that only the Lord's all-seeing eye could penetrate to the truth of the situation within the Ephesus church. Like an X-ray, he exposes the hidden weakness which their strengths obscured from human observers. His motivation for doing this is implicit in the description in Revelation 1 of the lampstands as golden. As we have remarked earlier, the church is not an organization but a living organism, indwelt by the Holy Spirit, permeated by the life of God. Only as such can she fulfil the true function which is to hold forth the light of Christ in the world. The lampstand does not exist for its own life but in order to be the means by which the light is spread. Since that light is Christ himself, the light of the world, the only worthy material of which the lampstand can possibly be constructed is gold. God is looking for gold in terms of character within his people and our congregations. If this is not there then he warns us that our place among the lampstands may well be forfeited. Verse 4 shows us that the gold for which he is looking is love.

We do not put this at the top of our own lists, do we? Why then is it so important to the Lord of the church? The answer must lie in the fact that love is the word that describes the relationship between God and his people. Deeper even than that, it is the nature of God himself. As John reminds us in his first letter, 'God is love' (1 Jn 4:8) and therefore one of the meanings of the mystery of the Trinity is that at the heart of God there is a dynamic interaction of love between the three persons. The biblical concept of God is not static or one-dimensional. The Trinity consists of each member loving the other in continuous perfection. That is why when God makes men in his own image, he makes us for relationships, first with himself as our Creator and then with our fellow men. Furthermore, he enshrines his Maker's instructions, in the two great commandments on which hang all the law and the prophets, as Jesus himself taught: "'Love the Lord your God with all your heart and with all your soul and with all your strength and with all your mind"; and, "love your neighbour as yourself"' (Lk 10:27). Love comes top on God's list of priorities.

Similarly, it is important to see that the root of sin is self-love. If we trace all the sins that spoil and mar our lives in this world back to their origin we discover that they have their roots in the refusal to give God the place he deserves in our lives. We want life to revolve around number one. At the heart of our rebellion against God there is an unwillingness to allow him to dictate to us what the priority should be, namely love. Thus, when God's salvation reaches us, it does so in the love of Calvary, the love demonstrated through the death of Jesus as he gave himself to the uttermost limit. It was, after all, to this very church at Ephesus that Paul wrote, 'Christ loved the church and gave himself up for her to make her holy . . . and to present her to himself as a radiant church, without stain or wrinkle or any other blemish, but holy and blameless' (Eph 5:25–27). If this is the heart of God's relationship with us, it is hardly surprising that he looks for our love in return. As John puts it, 'We love because he first loved us' (1 Jn 4:19). It is therefore important for us never to lose sight of the fact that our sin is basically a failure to love God and to love one another, love that he demands of those whom he has made in his own image.

When first we saw our sin and need, matched by the perfection of Christ's self-giving love on the cross, when first we received that full and free salvation which he offers, our whole lives were bound to him in gratitude and devotion, because of who he is and what he has done for us. This is the love that the Lord looks for in the church—first love. And if that is missing, it explains why everything else may be out of joint in our Christian lives.

But 'first love' describes not so much the time of that love as its quality. The phrase could equally be translated, and perhaps more helpfully, 'chief love'. It is the same word used in the parable of the prodigal son to describe the robe that the father insists on giving to the returning repentant younger son. He says this to his servants, 'Quick! Bring the *best* robe and put it on him' (Lk 15:22, italics mine). The Lord of the church is not simply looking for the renewed brightness of a baby Christian's experience. He is looking for the first place in our secret lives, what the Bible would call our hearts, and he is looking for that love to be demonstrated in all our relationships.

This is not designed to make us introspective, nor is it to encourage us to assess our spiritual health by the intensity of our feelings. Real love is seen in the completeness of our obedience. Dr Paul Reece once described this love (*agape*) as having 'a minimum of emotion and a maximum of evaluation'. The love for which the Lord is looking in our lives is not a warm feeling towards God, one that must ebb and flow with the tide, as every feeling does. We need rather to listen again to what Jesus said when he told his disciples, 'If you love me, you will obey what I command' (Jn 14:15). First love longs to do whatever the Lord whispers is his will. Again Jesus said, 'A new commandment I give you: Love one another. As I have loved you, so you must love one another' (Jn 13:34). First love is seen in a church where that kind of concern for one another animates one another. It is seen where Jesus is the centre of our affection and devotion, which we demonstrate not only in the words of our worship but in the obedience of our lives. It is demonstrated where Christians move at the impulse of his love, to carry out his will and to minister his grace. In such a community there will be an energy, enthusiasm and vitality that cannot be counterfeited.

Is it not that which many of our churches are missing? Look again at verse 4: 'You have *forsaken* your first love.' It is not that we have lost that love, but that we have left it. The Master's indictment is that there is a consciousness about our unwillingness to make him the chief love of our lives. It is not so much an accident as the result of deliberate choices. It is not just a fading away that is the product of time but a controlled movement that is the product of our wills. Real love grows. The contention that the Lord has with his church at Ephesus is that they have allowed a pattern of life to develop in which Christ has been squeezed into the margin of their lives.

If we are at all sensitive to the probing work of God's Holy Spirit we must surely recognize that the same can be very true of our own experience today. It is possible for us as Christians to be very active in God's service, working hard, dependable in our tasks, even self-sacrificing, and yet not to put our love for Christ as the first and most important reality of our lives. One of the devil's cleverest devices is to make us Christians worship our work rather than our Lord. It explains why there is so much empire building in church life today. It is fatally easy for us to make our ministries into our gods. All around us there is a multiplicity of Christian agencies vying for resources, trying to be bigger and better and more successful than others. Sadly there is often jealousy between the congregations and envy between churches. We may be busy about many things, but barren in our achievements. Therefore, our Christian service comes over as duty or, even worse, as drudgery. The reason would seem to be that we are not motivated by love for the Lord.

Similarly, we can be very correct in our ethical standards, and yet it is not love for the Lord that motivates us in this area so much as pride. We can uphold the highest moral standards on the grounds that we are not as other men are (Lk 18:11). If that pharasaism has crept into our thinking there will be a hardness towards those who fail and fall. We forget that we live by grace and that without Christ we have and are nothing. Moreover, we can have impeccable doctrinal standards, and be able to smell a heretic at a hundred yards, but our very correctness can be utterly hard and unloving. Even right and good things can be done in a wrong spirit. When I see Christians denouncing other believers for what they see as their unorthodoxy, I wonder how much love is in their hearts. You can contend for the faith in a spirit that actually denies the faith. Without love, correction will be bitterness, zeal will become hatred. Activity in the King's business will never make up for neglect of the King. That is why Paul wrote his great chapter on love in 1 Corinthians 13 and why the Lord of the church recalls the Ephesian Christians to the one essential, that which constitutes the bottom line.

If it is not true of us and our churches that we are progressing in love then Christ has something against us too. But verse 5 analyses for us how that situation has developed: 'Remember the height from which you have fallen! Repent and do the things you did at first.' Do you see what that tells us about true Christian love? It is known by actions. When you love someone, you want to spend time with them, you want to do all you can to please them, you are ready to give up yourself for them. They are at the very centre of your world. But the soil in which that plant grows is humility, submission and sacrifice. The problem at Ephesus was that they had ceased to do the things they did at first. The Lord was no longer the Chief or Number One in their consideration. They had adapted to an independent Christian lifestyle. We need to ask ourselves some searching questions about our own obedience. It is too easy for us to approximate Christ's commands to our level of commitment. Perhaps a good test question is to ask ourselves, 'What love-offering have I brought to the Lord Jesus in the recent past? What demonstration within my life have I made of my gratitude to him? Has there been any extravagance of devotion, any particular sacrifice by which I have said to him that he is my first love?'

Lastly, let us notice the change Christ demands. 'Demands' is not too strong a word, for the very future existence of this church is at stake: 'If you do not repent, I will come to you and remove your lampstand from its place' (verse 5b). We are not to understand this as a threat, but as a loving revelation of what will always happen if our first love is not Christ. Whether in the church or in our own personal discipleship, we shall stop loving one another and stop caring for the world. The Christian or a church that has no heart for mission, that has become concerned about its own inner power struggles and hardened into disputes and differences of opinion, and that is critical of others, is a Christian or a church that has left its love for Christ. His life and his light are no longer the dominant realities. By contrast, verse 7 speaks about the fulness of eternal life promised to those who overcome. The key question we must ask is how we are to be in that situation, rather than in the situation of the Ephesian church with its almost unrecognized compromise?

The text clearly shows us the changes that must be implemented in responding to Christ's demands. There are three steps back to usefulness. The first is to remember (verse 5a). That is a command that requires a conscious effort. The greatest danger is that we readily settle for our present mediocre level of Christian life and experience and write off anything better that we have known in the past as so much youthful enthusiasm. I meet many Christians who pride themselves on the fact that they are older and wiser now, but it can also mean that we are lazier and more stubborn. We need honestly to look at our love relationship with the Lord and ask ourselves whether there was not a time when it was deeper, fresher and more vibrant. Do not be prepared to settle for the status quo. Remember when things were better and try to find out those choices that have made the change. Remember too the love that the Lord Jesus has for you, for this is what we have fallen from when we have allowed him to be displaced from the central place in our affection. His love gave everything for us upon that cross, and as we remember that and personally feel the weight of his grace and his mercy, the Holy Spirit will stir us to want to be in that position of love towards the Lord Jesus which opens our lives to the riches of his forgiveness and his equipping power.

The second step is repentance: 'Repent and do the things you did at first' (verse 5b). Repentance is a change of mind that issues in a change of lifestyle. The Ephesian Christians were exhorted to go back to the attitude of total commitment to Christ that was theirs at first. Love is not a feeling that comes and goes; it is a conscious attitude of will that can be commanded. Repentance therefore is not remorse, which can simply be the expression of sadness at having been found out in our sin. Repentance signifies a resignation to the will of God and a casting of ourselves upon his mercy.

The story is told of how Admiral Lord Nelson received the surrender of a French admiral who had been conquered in one of his famous sea victories. The defeated admiral came on board Nelson's flagship in full ceremonial dress in order to make his surrender. He walked towards Nelson and put his hand out in order to shake Nelson's hand as a

sign of his recognition of Nelson's victory. But before
Nelson would shake his hand he requested him first to
hand over his sword. You cannot love the Lord until you
lay down your arms. It is as we are prepared to stop
fighting and let God be God in our lives that repentance
becomes genuine.

So whatever it is that has squeezed the Lord Jesus out of
the central place in our affections needs to be dealt with.
Whatever idols have been erected in his place, however
respectable or even spiritual they may be, they must be
removed and Christ re-established as our first love.

Thirdly, the final step back to usefulness is the step of
renewal: 'Do the things you did at first' (verse 5b).
Renewal is the other side of the coin of repentance. Our
commitment is expressed in action, the things that we do.
As we surrender our resistance to the will of God and as
we seek to remove the idols that crowd him out, we shall
need to confess to him our carelessness about cultivating
the love relationship with him for which he has redeemed
us. 'What must we do to do the works God requires?' the
Jewish crowd asked Jesus. His answer was clear: 'The
work of God is this: to believe in the one he has sent' (Jn
6:28, 29). If we really believe in him, we shall truly love
him. That is our part, enabled by his Spirit. His part is to
restore us and to pour into our lives the limitless love
which is the greatest characteristic of his nature.

'He who has an ear, let him hear what the Spirit says to
the churches' (verse 7a). The question remains with us as
individuals and as members of local congregations. Are we
prepared to listen to what God is saying and to respond to
the Spirit as he takes the word and applies it to our lives
and circumstances? If we want truly to understand our
church, we must begin with understanding ourselves. As
we see how much we are dependent upon the daily grace
of God, in Christ, and as we are thrilled by the marvellous
potential that opens up before us since the resources of

God are limitless and available to all who trust him for them, let us resolve to pray and work for and with our fellow Christians, asking God so to renew and empower his church in our generation that we become the people he intends us to be.

James Seddon's hymn says it all:

> Church of God, elect and glorious,
> Holy nation, chosen race;
> Called as God's own special people,
> Royal priests and heirs of grace:
> Know the purpose of your calling,
> Show to all his mighty deeds;
> Tell of love which knows no limits,
> Grace which meets all human needs.
>
> God has called you out of darkness
> Into his most marvellous light;
> Brought his truth to life within you,
> Turned your blindness into sight.
> Let your light so shine around you
> That God's name is glorified;
> And all find fresh hope and purpose
> In Christ Jesus crucified.
>
> Once you were an alien people,
> Strangers to God's heart of love;
> But he brought you home in mercy,
> Citizens of heaven above.
> Let his love flow out to others,
> Let them feel a father's care;
> That they too may know his welcome
> And his countless blessings share.
>
> Church of God, elect and holy,
> Be the people he intends;

Strong in faith and swift to answer
Each command your Master sends:
Royal priests, fulfil your calling
Through your sacrifice and prayer;
Give your lives in joyful service—
Sing his praise, his love declare.

(No. 504 in *Hymns for Today's Church*
published by Hodder & Stoughton)

Understanding Jesus
Who Jesus is and why he matters

by Alister McGrath

You may know something about Jesus. You may even know and love him as your Saviour. But do you understand the *significance* of what he came to do?

This book offers the believer a clear reason for the faith that is within him, while to the enquirer it explains simply and clearly what Christians believe and why.

'I welcome this book most enthusiastically. It is an excellent excample of profundity married to simplicity.'

> MICHAEL GREEN
> Professor of Evangelism
> Regent College, Vancouver
> (formerly Rector, St Aldate's, Oxford)

'It will help us to understand more about the Christ who is at the centre of our faith.'

> JOHN B. TAYLOR
> Bishop of St Albans

Dr. ALISTER McGRATH is the author of several major scholarly works. This is his first book for a wider readership, in which his gift of clear expression is used to the full. At present he teaches theology at Wycliffe Hall, Oxford, where he lives with his wife Joanna and two small children.

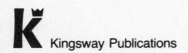

Kingsway Publications

Understanding The Trinity

by Alister McGrath

How can we talk about God when he is beyond the grasp of human understanding?

Down through the ages Christians have looked for ways of talking about their experience of the Living God without doing an injustice to his majesty and infinity. One result has been the curious – some would say baffling – doctrine of the Trinity: God the Father, Son and Holy Spirit.

Alister McGrath's earlier book on *Understanding Jesus* was hailed as a rare example of a theologian talking in plain terms about Christian claims and teaching. In *Understanding the Trinity* Dr McGrath writes with equal clarity, as he shows that the doctrine of the Trinity has been the only adequate response that the church has made to God's revelation of himself in history.

The Rev. Dr. ALISTER McGRATH is a member of the Oxford University Faculty of Theology, and teaches theology at Wycliffe Hall. His earlier scientific training adds an extra dimension to his writing, giving rise to a logical and down-to-earth presentation of ideas.

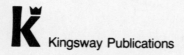

Kingsway Publications

Build That Bridge

by David Coffey

The last twenty years have witnessed some significant moves towards visible Christian unity. It is no longer possible to label a Christian by his church name and then confidently suppose that you know his every belief and attitude. The church—the whole church—is in ferment, and barriers are being shaken.

Yet there is still division.

David Coffey seeks to bring the guidance of a pastor's heart into two aspects of that division:

— first, he asks Christians within the same local church to face renewal and change without needless division or carnal schism:

— secondly, he asks church leaders to be prepared to talk to each other across the varying divides in a spirit of mutual recognition.

This is a book that asks searching questions, but never leaves us without a hope of an answer.

'I heartily commend this admirable and timely book. It is, in my view, well written, warm, almost passionate in tone, always interesting, very fair and genuinely open'.

PHILIP GREENSLADE
The King's Church, Aldershot

'May this be a launching pad to send folk exploring regions beyond where even this far-sighted author hoped to send them'.

COLIN BUCHANAN
Bishop of Aston

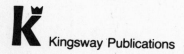

Kingsway Publications